African American Teens Discuss Their Schooling Experiences

Gail L. Thompson

BERGIN & GARVEY
Westport, Connecticut • London

Library of Congress Cataloging-in-Publication Data

Thompson, Gail L., 1957–
    African American teens discuss their schooling experiences / Gail L. Thompson.
        p. cm.
    Includes bibliographical references (p.) and index.
    ISBN 0-89789-843-5 (alk. paper)
        1. African Americans—Education. 2. African American high school
    students—Attitudes. 3. Educational surveys—United States.   I.   Title.
    LC2717.T47 2002
    373.1829'96'073—dc21   2001037915

British Library Cataloguing in Publication Data is available.

Library of Congress Catalog Card Number: 2001037915
ISBN: 0-89789-843-5

First published in 2002

Bergin & Garvey, 88 Post Road West, Westport, CT 06881
An imprint of Greenwood Publishing Group, Inc.
www.greenwood.com

Printed in the United States of America

The paper used in this book complies with the
Permanent Paper Standard issued by the National
Information Standards Organization (Z39.48-1984).

10 9 8 7 6 5 4 3 2 1

Contents

Tables	vii
Preface	ix
Acknowledgments	xi
Introduction	xiii
Part I: Elementary School Experiences	**1**
1 Elementary School as a Precursor to Subsequent Schooling Experiences	3
2 Early Reading Habits and Attitudes about Reading	17
3 Elementary Teachers	31
4 Elementary Course Work and Homework	45
Part II: Middle School Experiences	**57**
5 Middle School Issues	59
6 Middle School Teachers	69
7 Middle School Course Work and Homework	79
Part III: High School Experiences	**89**
8 High School as an Ending and a Beginning	91
9 High School Teachers	99
10 High School Course Work and Homework	109
Part IV: Other Issues	**121**
11 Attitudes about College and Future Plans	123
12 Racism at School	133
13 School Safety	141

Contents

14 Parent Involvement   151
15 Conclusion   161

References   169

Index   175

Tables

3-1 Qualities of Outstanding Educators   33

3-2 Grades in Which Students Had Their Best Elementary
      Teachers   35

3-3 Grades in Which Students Had Their Worst Elementary
      Teachers   36

4-1 Grades in Which Students Had Their Most Difficult
      Elementary Course Work   46

4-2 Grades in Which Students Had Their Easiest Elementary
      Course Work   47

4-3 How Students Rated the Overall Quality of Instruction
      Provided by Most of Their Elementary Teachers   48

4-4 The Number of Days per Week That Students Received
      Homework during Elementary School   49

4-5 The Number of Hours per Week That Students Spent on
      Homework Assignments during Elementary School   50

4-6 How Students Rated the Benefits of Their Elementary
      School Homework   51

6-1 Best Middle School Teachers   70

6-2 Worst Middle School Teachers   71

7-1 The Most Difficult Middle School Courses for Students   80

7-2 The Easiest Middle School Courses for Students   80

7-3 How Students Rated the Quality of Instruction Provided by
      Their Middle School Teachers   81

7-4 The Number of Days per Week That Students Received
      Homework during Middle School   82

7-5 The Number of Hours per Week That Students Spent on
          Homework Assignments during Middle School   83
7-6 How Students Rated the Benefits of Their Middle School
          Homework   83
9-1 Best High School Teachers   100
9-2 Worst High School Teachers   102
9-3 Students' Perceptions of Their Teachers' Expectations and
          Beliefs about Them   103
10-1 High School Courses That Students Failed   110
10-2 The Most Difficult High School Courses   110
10-3 The Easiest High School Courses   111
10-4 How Students Rated the Quality of Instruction Provided
          by Most of Their Ninth Grade Teachers   111
10-5 How Students Rated the Quality of Instruction Provided
          by Most of Their Tenth Grade Teachers   112
10-6 How Students Rated the Quality of Instruction Provided
          by Most of Their Eleventh Grade Teachers   113
10-7 How Students Rated the Quality of Instruction Provided
          by Most of Their Twelfth Grade Teachers   113
10-8 The Number of Days per Week That Students Received
          Homework during High School   114
10-9 The Number of Hours per Week That Students Spent on
          Homework Assignments during High School   115
10-10 How Students Rated the Benefits of Their High School
          Homework   116
11-1 How Public Schools Can Better Prepare Students for
          College   129
12-1 The Culprit(s) of the Racism That Students Experienced
          at Their High Schools   136
14-1 How Students Rated Their Parents'/Guardians'
          Involvement in Their Elementary School Education   154
14-2 How Students Rated Their Parents'/Guardians'
          Involvement in Their Middle School Education   155
14-3 How Students Rated Their Parents'/Guardians'
          Involvement in Their High School Education   155

Preface

During the 1999–2000 academic year, I collected data from 271 African American high school seniors at seven high schools in five different school districts in Southern California. The purpose of the study was to give these students an opportunity to discuss many aspects of their K–12 schooling experiences. At a time when African American students nationwide often have less positive schooling experiences than students from mainstream backgrounds, feedback from African American students might improve the situation. This book is intended to give educators and educational policymakers a candid look into the personal and school-related lives of these students. It is an attempt to alleviate cultural misunderstandings between African American students and educators and also an opportunity for these students to speak from their hearts.

Acknowledgments

First, I thank God for an opportunity to share a message that will hopefully improve the schooling experiences of African American students nationwide. This study would not have been possible without the assistance of numerous individuals. I am deeply grateful to the 271 African American students who completed the questionnaire and the 28 students who participated in the interview phase of the study. I am also grateful to the teachers, principals, parents, and school district officials who gave me permission to distribute the questionnaire and to conduct interviews. Moreover, I am extremely thankful and appreciative of the support of my husband, Rufus Thompson, and my children, Nafissa, NaChe', and Stephen Thompson, who provided me with great encouragement and assisted me with proofreading the manuscript. I am also grateful to my mother, Velma Coleman; sisters Tracy Smith and Michelle Harris, my aunt Ebbie Crear and cousin Brenda Kelly; Miriam Avila, my student assistant for inputting surveys, transcribing interviews, and proofreading; my niece TreaAndrea Russworm for proofreading and providing useful feedback; my good friends Malinda West, Cynthia Hebron, Wanda Foster, Sharon Holmes-Johnson, Margaret Goss, Dorothea Williams, Carolyn McCauley, Pamela Merchant-Guidry, Angel Roberts, Gloria Porter, Dr. Barbara Flores, Dr. Camille Mayers, Dr. Marilyn Joshua-Shearer, Dr. Maria Balderrama, Dr. June Hetzel, Dwayne and Ardelia Rhone, Deborah Murray, and Dr. Angela Louque; mentors Gloria Pearley, Ed Cray, Dr. David Drew, Dr. Lourdes Arguelles, Dr. Bruce Matsui, and Dr. Judith Jackson for believing in all my writing projects and for providing me with great encouragement; and to Dr. Asa G. Hilliard III and Dr. James P. Comer, eminent African

American scholars, for agreeing—without knowing me personally—to take time out of their busy schedules to read this book and provide important feedback. Finally, I am thankful to Jane Garry and the staff at Greenwood Publishing Group for believing in this project and for being extremely supportive.

Introduction

During the last two years, I have been inundated with calls for help from teachers, administrators, school district officials, and parents. Most of the parents have been African Americans. The common theme running through our conversations has been "What can I do to improve the way that my child is treated by teachers and administrators at school?" The common theme from educators is "What can be done to improve achievement levels of minority children, particularly African Americans?" The quietest, yet strongest, cries for help, however, have come either directly from African American students themselves or indirectly from others who spoke on their behalf.

The following examples are stories that have been shared with me and that served as the catalyst for this book. Each story contains the same message. Whether subtle or overt, the message is that in spite of all of the progress that has been made to improve race relations in America and to improve schooling conditions for all children, there is still much work to be done. Some of this work entails improving the schooling experiences of African American children by challenging deficit mind-sets and theories, and by offering additional strategies and perspectives to educators. But first we must be willing to listen to other voices that have traditionally been silenced, discounted, and disparaged. Instead of only listening to researchers, policymakers, educators, and other "experts," we must turn a receptive ear to the voices of students who have been historically marginalized.

STORIES FROM AND ABOUT AFRICAN AMERICAN STUDENTS

Last year, I heard an African American college undergraduate complain, "When I was in school, the only things they taught me about my culture were Slavery and Martin Luther King Jr." A few months earlier, a friend of mine, who has three African American children in a predominantly White Los Angeles County elementary school, telephoned me. She was exasperated with educators at her children's school. On a number of occasions, educators had exhibited what appeared to be signs of cultural insensitivity and cultural ignorance. In one case, a third grade teacher assigned a report on "A Famous American Explorer." When one of the African American boys in the predominantly White class said that he wanted to do his report on a famous African American explorer, the teacher told him that there was no such thing. When the child's parents complained to the principal, the principal asked, "Well, were there ever any Black explorers?" It appears that both the principal and teacher were unaware that Matthew Henson, a Black man, "discovered" the North Pole, along with Admiral Robert Peary.

Since then, this same parent and I have had numerous conversations. Each time, she has expressed frustration over her children's experiences at school. For example, on several occasions she has been upset by the way her daughter, a first grader who has cerebral palsy and who is the only African American child in the class, has been treated by the teacher or the instructional aide. The child has no friends in the class and often cries about comments that other children make, such as "I can't play with you because you're a brown girl." In spite of the fact that this first grader has been ostracized by her classmates merely because she is of a different race and has a physical disability, the teacher has told the parent that it is really no big deal. The saddest commentary of all is that when this child started school, she was enthusiastic. Now, she literally hates school and dreads going.

Another African American parent, who is also an educator, told me that she decided to move her son, a middle school student, to another school district. "One of his seventh grade teachers basically destroyed his self-esteem," she said. "He's just now starting to recover from the damage. I went to school administrators and district officials, but nothing was done. I decided that it was best to move my child to an entirely different district, so that he could start over," she stated.

Last year, I telephoned an African American ninth grader that I was mentoring at a local high school. When I asked how she was doing in school, her frustration became evident. "I don't understand *Romeo and Juliet*," she complained. Her English teacher had assigned a portion of *Romeo and Juliet* for homework, and the student was struggling to comprehend the play. When she told the teacher that she was having difficulty, the teacher told her that perhaps the real problem was that the girl was lazy. On the contrary, this ninth grader was not only determined to eventually go to college, but she was also striving to get outstanding grades in all her classes. Instead of modifying her instructional practices or suggesting alternatives that might make the play more comprehensible, the teacher assumed that the student, not the difficulty of interpreting anachronistic Shakespearean English, was the problem. The question that I've pondered is, "If a White student had told the teacher that she was struggling to understand Shakespeare, would the teacher have assumed that the student was lazy?"

One of my Latina students in a college reading course that I was teaching shared another story with me. One day, her biracial (half-Black, half-Mexican) son complained to her that there were no books about Black children in his kindergarten classroom library. His mother suggested that he should mention this to his teacher. When the boy went to school, he told his teacher that he loved reading the "Little Bill" series, colorful and humorous short-chapter books written by Bill Cosby, that his mother had purchased for him. He asked the teacher if these books could be added to the classroom library. The teacher told him that the books were for first graders and that he would have to wait until the following year to read them at school. Unfortunately, she did not or could not suggest other books about African Americans that could be added to the kindergarten classroom library in order to quench this child's desire to read books that he could relate to.

One of the most disturbing stories was shared with me by a White vice principal who serves on a local diversity committee with me. Several months ago, he invited me to visit his elementary school. This predominantly White school has no Black teachers, few male teachers, and only a couple of Hispanic teachers, even though children of color account for 80 percent of the students in the school district.

Before this vice principal was hired, the school had an extremely high suspension and expulsion rate for African American children (which remains a problem in the school district as a whole). This vice principal, however, reduced the suspension and expulsion rate for African American children at his school by discouraging teachers from "making mountains out of molehills" and teaching them alternative strategies to use in dealing with minor problems. But last year, an incident occurred that still has him flabbergasted.

One day, he saw two police officers approaching the school. He was shocked to learn that a teacher had telephoned the police, saying that her life was in danger. It turned out that an African American boy in the teacher's classroom had kicked a chair. As a result, the teacher feared that he was going to kill her, so she telephoned the police. The child was a tall first grader, but a first grader nonetheless. As the vice principal concluded the story, he told me, "White kids kick chairs all of the time at this school and nobody calls the police, but if a Black boy does it, it's a different story."

On another occasion, after deciding to become a mentor at this same elementary school, I went to the school to work on literacy activities with four students in kindergarten, first grade, and second grade. At least two of these students were in danger of being retained in their current grade. Three of the four had also been labeled as "discipline problems."

When I arrived at the school on the day in question, three of the four students were either in Detention or on "Time Out." In other words, they had been sent out of class as a result of some problem or conflict. When I asked one of the students, why he had been placed on "Time Out," he said that his teacher had asked the class to do an arithmetic problem and then told them to add the number five to the problem. When the boy blurted out, "Dang! This is hard!" the teacher sent him out of class. At the time when this incident occurred, this African American boy was a five-year-old kindergartner. He was inquisitive and quite smart, but the wheels that would almost guarantee that he would be retained in kindergarten were already in motion.

Thereafter, I witnessed or heard about other incidents between him and the teacher. On another day, the boy's older sister—a sixth grader—told me that his teacher had sent him out of class and later told his mother that she had no idea how to handle a child who is so outspoken and that she felt that the boy was disrespectful. Later, I heard the teacher scolding him and saying, "This doesn't make any sense at all. Go pull your card!" It turned out that the child had been tying his shoe when the teacher called roll that morning and didn't hear her call his name. The teacher assumed that he was being defiant. As a result, he was punished. On several occasions, this student was in the classroom for less than 15 minutes before the teacher kicked him out for some "infraction."

Another story that served as a catalyst for this book involves a group of African American high school seniors who were members of a local church. In an effort to reward high school seniors for their educational accomplishments, the church sponsors an annual scholarship banquet. In order to earn a scholarship, each high school senior must submit an application. The application requires seniors to include their grade point average, record of extracurricular school involvement, and community service. Students earn points based on a rubric. Each year, on the day of the banquet, students and their families gather for a time of celebration to honor the scholarship recipients. When the scholarship banquet was held during the summer of 1999, all of the female high school seniors received a scholarship. It turned out, however, that not one of the African American male seniors was eligible for a scholarship, because not one of them had enough credits even to graduate.

INQUIRIES FROM ADMINISTRATORS

Whereas parents and African American students have shared stories with me expressing frustration over negative schooling experiences, I have noticed that the common thread that runs through most of the inquiries that I receive from administrators is "What can we do to improve the academic performance of African American children?" One of the causes of the heightened interest in African American children is new legislation from the California Department of Education (CDE), mandating higher teaching standards and more accountability.

In 1999, the California Public Schools Accountability Act (PSAA) was approved by the legislature and signed by the governor. One of the components of the PSAA is the Academic Performance Index (API), which uses students' standardized test scores to rate schools on a scale of 200–1000. The state's target is 800. Each school is expected to show at least a 5 percent improvement each year. Low-performing schools who do not show improvement run the risk of being taken over by the state. High-performing schools become eligible for monetary rewards. Just as there is pressure on school administrators and teachers, there is also tremendous pressure on students. Students who fail to meet certain standards are likely to be retained. Moreover, students will also be required to take a high school exit exam in the near future. These developments do not bode well for African American elementary and secondary students, for in most cases, when API scores are disaggregated by race/ethnicity, the scores of Black children are at the very bottom.

CALIFORNIA AS A TRENDSETTER

Events that affect California's educational system are important on a national level for several reasons. California's K–12 students populate the nation's largest and most ethnically diverse public school system. As a result, California is one of the states that sets trends for textbook markets (Manzo, 1997a; Routman, 1996), and California has historically been considered to be a trendsetter of educational policy. Furthermore, what happens in California is often indicative of what is happening in other states. In a recent example, California outlawed affirmative action and states such as Michigan and Texas attempted to follow suit. Moreover, issues relating to literacy in California are issues that are being wrestled with in many states throughout the nation.

AN AGE-OLD PROBLEM

For decades, many researchers have attempted to ascertain why disproportionately high percentages of Black children lag behind their peers of other races in school. Although much finger-pointing—including the common solution of blaming the victim (Hale, 1986)—still occurs, an increasing body of literature points to the important role of the teacher in fostering literacy and providing students with a strong academic foundation.

Nearly four decades ago, Clark (1965) argued that because African American children are disparaged, disrespected, and relegated to an inferior status in schools, they develop contempt for their teachers and the educational system. The results are high dropout rates and discipline problems. The real culprit, according to Clark, is a cultural clash between poor children and their teachers. Clark concluded that the weak academic performance of many African American children is caused by ineffective teaching methods and "educational default." More recently, Hare and Hare (1991) made a similar point.

Hacker (1992), Joseph (1996), and Oakes (1990) maintained that the inability of many teachers to recognize that some African American children possess different learning styles from White children has been detrimental to countless African American children. Joseph (1996) found that poor African American students are more likely to be punished or retained in a grade than are White students. Like Clark (1965), she blamed the educational system.

Comer and Poussaint (1992), Hale (1986), and Morgan (1980) described how a substantial number of African American children, particularly boys, were being medicated upon the advice of teachers who felt that the students were uncontrollable. Several studies have also shown that a preponderance of children who are labeled as "problem children, uneducable, defiant, or aggressive" are minority children, and African American boys in particular. One viewpoint is that this common trend is not accidental or based on ignorance on the teachers' part, but on an actual conspiracy that is designed to destroy African American boys (Kunjufu, 1985).

One of the most obvious ways in which the educational system has been detrimental to African American children is through tracking, the practice of sorting children into different academic groups or "tracks." A disproportionate number of African American and Hispanic children are placed in lower-level academic tracks instead of college preparatory tracks (Hacker, 1992; Oakes, 1999). Conversely, African American children are overrepresented in Special Education classes (Hacker, 1992). Ford (1995) noted that whereas African American children are overrepresented in Special Education classes (Hale, 1986), they are severely underrepresented in classes for "gifted" children. Mitchell (1982) and Oakes (1999) found that even when they had similar standardized test scores, African American children were less likely than White children to be placed in higher academic tracks. This underrepresentation stems from placement criteria that may be biased against students with non-traditional learning styles. Drew (1996) illustrated how girls and students from minority groups are often discouraged from taking challenging science and math courses, which in the long run decreases the number of fields in which they will be able to major.

Another way in which the educational system has failed African American children is through its disparagement of their linguistic codes (Labov, 1972). Johnson (1969) said that in addition to the methods and materials that are used to teach African American children Standard English, an unwillingness on the part of educators to recognize Black English as fundamentally different from Standard English has caused the poor school performance of African American children. Smither-man (1977) cited teachers' ignorance of African American speech patterns as one of the main reasons so many African American children are labeled as "functionally illiterate." Darder (1991) said that "language domination" still occurs in schools because bicultural students infer that their primary languages are deemed inferior and also because traditional instructional approaches foster subordinate social relations. The result is that their voices are silenced in the classroom. Delpit (1995) also described how the voices of bicultural children have been silenced in classrooms through teachers' prejudices toward their primary languages and also the use of destructive instructional practices. Like other researchers, she noted that teachers are more likely to overcorrect speakers of Black English and thereby stifle their enthusiasm. This has also made it less likely for these children to learn Standard English because their "affective filter" becomes blocked.

In spite of the negative conclusions that many researchers have reached regarding the schooling experiences of African American youths, the fact remains that many African Americans have used the educational system to improve the quality of their lives. Nevertheless, disproportionately high numbers of African American elementary and secondary school students continue to lag behind their peers of other races.

In states such as California where stringent measures, in the form of high-stakes testing, have been taken to improve public schools, there is great cause for alarm. Because African American students traditionally have not done as well on standardized tests as their counterparts, they are in greater danger of being retained and of failing to receive a high school diploma. A substantial body of research indicates that there are strong correlations between grade retention and school dropout rates.

Additionally, the lack of a high school diploma is related to future economic, social, and educational mobility. Wilson (1996) found that poor and minority children are more likely than others to have underprepared teachers, substitute teachers, and teachers who are teaching out of their area of expertise. Moreover, many researchers have found that teachers tend to have lower expectations for minority children than they do for White children (Au, 1993). Comer and Poussaint (1992) and Hare and Hare (1991) concluded that the educational system has prepared African American children for menial and subservient roles in society. Darder (1991) said that less than 10 percent of low-income minority students will be able to improve their socioeconomic status. Furthermore, in the United States, African American children are already more likely than any other group of children to be living in poverty (U.S. Census Bureau, 2000). For many children, education is the only legitimate vehicle by which they may improve the quality of their lives (Drew, 1996).

AN ALTERNATIVE: LISTENING TO AND LEARNING FROM THE VOICES OF AFRICAN AMERICAN STUDENTS

There is clearly a need for alternatives that will improve the academic achievement levels of African American students. Although the topic of African American school achievement has been explored by many researchers, very little research has permitted African American students to speak on their own behalf and to offer suggestions, as the true experts on their own experiences. This book attempts to do so by describing schooling experiences of African American students through data that were collected from the students themselves. In an effort to help teachers—particularly new teachers—administrators, and policymakers find ways to improve achievement levels of African American students, this book describes numerous aspects of the K–12 schooling experiences of African American students.

In order to successfully teach African American students, it is imperative that teachers have some knowledge of African American culture (Hale, 1986). Most teachers come from backgrounds that are extremely different from that of their African American students (Hare & Hare, 1991; Hooks, 1989; Smitherman, 1977). Because most news coverage about African Americans is negative (Chideya, 1995), cultural ignorance is inevitable. Furthermore, research about African Americans has historically been negative (Chideya, 1995; Delpit, 1995; Hacker, 1992; White & Parham, 1990). A teacher who has a negative perception of African Americans will undoubtedly create a hostile or uncomfortable classroom environment and become ineffective. If students perceive that their teacher is fearful of them, some will take advantage and become disruptive. Others may "shut down" academically. Moreover, as a result of class-size reductions, massive teacher shortages have occurred, as in California. Many underprepared individuals are now teaching in classrooms. In 2000, for example, the California State Department of Education reported that more than 30,000 California teachers were working under Emergency Credentials. Some of these teachers had not yet taken any teacher training courses.

Much of the research indicates that teachers play an invaluable role in literacy acquisition and the academic success or failure of African American students. Because many teachers are culturally insensitive and underprepared to work with African American children and use ineffective instructional practices, these teachers unwittingly serve as deterrents to academic achievement. Overreliance on standardized tests (Gould, 1981) and tracking have been detrimental to minority students. Moreover, the prevailing attitude in numerous schools throughout the nation stems from the belief that it is okay for educators to give minority and poor children a "watered down" curriculum. Substandard schooling has far-reaching consequences that become most evident in the disproportionate number of African Americans who make up America's poor and who are underprepared for university course work.

Research that is based on feedback from African American students is timely and imperative. This is a period when (1) African American student enrollment has plummeted at University of California institutions and in other states where there has been an anti-affirmative action backlash; (2) numerous state institutions, such as the California State University system, have curtailed remedial education programs; (3) standardized test scores of African American and Hispanic elementary and secondary school students continue to lag behind those of their White and Asian peers; and (4) social promotion is being eradicated in many school districts. As fewer individuals from non-mainstream backgrounds choose teaching as a profession, and Whites predominate in the field of education, "academic standoffs" (Orange & Horowitz, 1999) and cultural misunderstandings are likely to proliferate. This book can become extremely beneficial in adding to the existing body of literature regarding the schooling experiences of African American students.

METHOD

Two data sets were collected from students through a questionnaire and interviews. Judd, Smith, and Kidder (1991) found that the use of more than one method to gather data may improve data quality. They also stated that the use of questionnaires is one way to reduce interviewer bias that is associated with the use of interviews. Among other benefits, they noted that questionnaires provide more anonymity and decrease the discomfort that might stem from having to answer questions of a sensitive nature. A final reason why two methods were used to gather data is that at the outset of the current study, it was assumed that numerous positive associations between the questionnaire results and the interview results would become apparent.

The Questionnaire

Officials in seven high schools in five school districts in two contiguous counties agreed to participate in the study. Both counties have extremely low college attendance rates. One thousand nine hundred eighty-three high school seniors handed in questionnaires. All students completed the surveys in their English, psychology, or government classes. Hispanics, Whites, and African Americans, respectively, were the three largest groups of respondents. The current study, however, focuses solely on data from the 271 African American students. Data from the other students will be used in future research projects.

Reliability was increased by the length of the questionnaire, and multiple questions were included to ensure that internal consistency occurred (Judd et al., 1991). There were 59 questions and a section for additional comments. Another strategy to increase reliability was to include more than one question about the dependent variables (Kerlinger, 1986). Validity was ensured through field testing the instrument. Moreover, the questionnaire was reviewed and approved by a university Institutional Review Board. The questionnaire can be divided into four broad categories: elementary school experiences, middle school experiences, high school experiences, and other issues.

Interviews

The second data set was based on interviews. Interviews are important for several reasons (Judd et al., 1991). They are more conducive to eliciting elaboration, and they also require more time than that required by questionnaire completion (Kerlinger, 1986). Twenty-eight African American high school seniors participated in the interview phase. There were 16 females and 12 males from four schools in two different districts. These students were selected from a survey item that stated, "If you would like to be interviewed in order to provide more information for the study, please include your name and telephone number." Although a total of 48 African American students indicated that they wanted to be interviewed, some students could not be interviewed for one or more of the following reasons: (1) They failed to hand in a Parent Consent form; (2) they were absent from school on the days when interviews were conducted at their school site; or (3) school administrators would not agree to permit them to participate in the interview phase of the study. Interviewees were asked to provide more details about the survey questions and also several additional questions regarding school safety, suspensions, expulsions, teacher expectations and attitudes, sexual harassment, and their future plans. All interviews were recorded on audiocassette.

Analysis

The surveys were analyzed through a statistical software program. Univariate and bivariate statistics were examined. Intertextual analysis was used to interpret the interview results. Recurring themes and direct quotes that respond to key questions will be reported.

THE BOOK'S ORGANIZATION

This book is organized into four main sections: Elementary School Experiences, Middle School Experiences, High School Experiences, and Other Issues. To provide a context and pertinent background information about issues that are addressed in the chapter, most chapters begin with a review of related literature. Many chapters also include detailed narratives from students who were interviewed as well as data from the questionnaire results. In order to present a "complete" portrait of students' K–12 schooling experiences, the narratives are organized chronologically, starting with elementary school and continuing through secondary school to show how different levels of schooling are related. Therefore, even in the elementary school section, for example, the narratives include information about middle school and high school; and similarly in the middle school and high school sections of the book. Additionally, for several sections of the book, comparisons are made according to the elementary tracks that students were in and whether or not they were retained during elementary school, to ascertain if their academic tracks or retention had any bearing on the quality of their schooling experiences and their related attitudes.

Chapter 1 illustrates why the elementary school experiences are precursors to future schooling experiences. Chapter 2 describes the students' early reading habits and attitudes about reading. Chapter 3 presents information about the students' elementary teachers, characteristics of good teachers, how they rated their teachers, and their teachers' attitudes and expectations of them. In chapter 4, the students share important information about their elementary school course work and homework and whether or not they found this work to be benefi-cial. Chapter 5 presents background information and pertinent snap-shots of the students' middle school experiences. Chapter 6 offers information about their middle school teachers. In chapter 7, the stu-dents discuss issues relating to their middle school course work and homework. Chapter 8 presents the students' high school experiences as both an ending and a beginning. In chapter 9, the students talk exten-sively about their high school teachers. In chapter 10, students discuss aspects of their high school course work and homework. In chapter 11, students share their attitudes about college, whether or not they felt that they were adequately prepared for college, and their future plans. Chapter 12 delves into numerous issues relating to racism at school. Chapter 13 focuses on issues pertaining to school safety. Chapter 14 discusses parent involvement at the elementary, middle school, and high school levels. Chapter 15 provides a summary of key findings, concluding remarks, and recommendations for policymakers, teacher training institutions, school counselors, and teachers.

Part I

Elementary School Experiences

Elementary School as a Precursor to Subsequent Schooling Experiences

Starting school is a major milestone for most children. The first and last years of school, in particular, are probably the most memorable of all school years. During the first year, crucial decisions are made about children's aptitude. Often at this time labels are placed on children that remain with them for the duration of their years in school. Some children get put into the "smart" group; others are placed in the "dumb" group. As Shannon (1992) noted, these groups can determine which academic track children are eventually placed in. Prior to the 1970s, researchers assumed that most children were basically the same (Comer & Poussaint, 1992; Wilson, 1987). As a result, the same standards were used to measure cognitive, physiological, and educational growth, and the middle-class White child became the standard used for benchmarks (Wilson, 1987). This standard resulted in deficit views of African American children. In most ways, they were deemed to be inferior to middle-class White children.

Although deficit views of African American children are still common (Ladson-Billings, 1994), in recent years some researchers have argued that there are fundamental differences between African American and White children and these differences cannot be ignored. Moreover, these differences result in qualitatively different life experiences and ways of viewing the world, and they create a special set of problems for African Americans that affect their schooling experiences. The primary source of these differences is racism, which affects most aspects of African Americans' lives, development, and viewpoint of society (Comer & Poussaint, 1992).

For African American children and other children from bicultural backgrounds, entering school for the first time can be similar to visiting a foreign land. Mismatches between the home and school environment can have far-reaching consequences. In *Black Children: Their Roots, Culture, and Learning Styles* (1986), Hale emphasized the important role that early childhood education can play in the lives of African American children. Because these children must "master" at least two cultures, both parents and teachers must help them "straddle" these cultures.

Kozol (1986), Kunjufu (1985), and Morgan (1980) revealed a paradox: African American children who enter school with outstanding potential and a thirst for learning undergo a negative transformation that manifests itself during fourth grade. White and Parham (1990) said that although African American children start school with skills that are equal to those of their White counterparts, the longer they are in school, the more their achievement levels decline. Foster and Peele (1999) said that as early as second grade, African American boys are already "haunted" by the fact that they are portrayed negatively in American society.

During her study of 200 predominately White and Asian students who were enrolled in an undergraduate psychology course, Murray (1996) researched how teachers evaluate students. After viewing a videotape of four children and reading background information about their parents, the subjects evaluated the children. The results showed that race, gender, and class were strong determinants of how the children were evaluated. The subjects assumed that the African American child in the video was less intelligent than the White child. Murray found race to be the main determinant of how the children were evaluated. Consequently, the Black child received the lowest evaluation in each area, and the White child received the highest.

In addition to myriad school-related problems, such as retention, tracking, cultural conflicts, and the like, that students may experience during the elementary school years, many students come from less than ideal home environments. Poverty, for example, has far-reaching effects. Because a high percentage of African American children live in poverty, there is a great likelihood that these children will enter school with some of the issues relating to poverty. W.J. Wilson (1996) noted that there are major differences between the lives of the "working poor" and the lives of the "unemployed poor." A discussion that occurred in a graduate course taught by the author of the current study reveals the prevalence of poverty in many schools but also that attitudes regarding children from impoverished backgrounds differ among teachers.

During the class discussion, the question of what teachers should do when children come to school complaining of hunger arose. One elementary teacher turned up her nose and replied, "I don't think that it's my job to feed other people's children." Another teacher said, "I don't want to hear anything about the kids' home lives." Another teacher answered, "I got tired of my students saying 'I'm hungry.' So I went to the 99 Cents Store and purchased juice and crackers. Now, when they say that they're hungry, I feed them."

What became evident during the discussion is that although there are free and reduced breakfast and lunch programs at most schools, if a child who is eligible for the free or reduced breakfast and lunch program arrives at school late, he/she misses breakfast. Therefore, the child must remain hungry until lunch time or until a teacher finds an alternative, as did the teacher who was willing to spend a few dollars keeping her classroom supplied with food. Like all good teachers, she realized that it is impossible to "feed the mind" when the stomach is empty. This teacher realized what Abraham Maslow revealed many years ago: If basic needs, such as food, shelter, and safety have not been met first, higher-level needs, such as intellectual achievement, cannot be met (Eggen & Kauchak, 2001).

Another problem relating to poverty is that children who live in impoverished areas are also more likely than children from mainstream and those of a higher socioeconomic status to be exposed to crime and violence. Garbarino et al. (1992) conducted a study and found that high percentages of children living in urban areas of the United States are suffering from post-traumatic stress disorder, as a result of exposure to trauma and violence. They concluded, however, that with the right attitude and effective instructional practices, teachers can become successful with these students.

The African American students who participated in the current study were asked numerous questions about their elementary school experiences. Ninety-seven percent of the students attended elementary school in California. Some students attended a kindergarten through fifth grade elementary school, and others attended a school that included sixth grade. Most were in basic elementary classes. About 21 percent were placed in the Gifted and Talented Education program (G.A.T.E.), and 4 percent were placed in Special Education classes. Ten percent of the students were retained at least once in elementary school. Most of the students who were retained repeated either kindergarten or second grade. Special Education students comprised 67 percent of the retained students.

The students who participated in the current study resided in an area that has a high unemployment rate, high child-poverty rate, and one of the lowest college attendance rates in the state. Students who participated in the interview phase of the study were asked if they experienced any obstacles or problems during elementary school that might have made it difficult for them to succeed in life. Although many of these students came from impoverished backgrounds, most said that they did not experience any major problem or obstacle. Those who did, however, shared a variety of examples of problems. Some were associated with poverty, and some were associated with normal childhood experiences. For example, many students were deeply affected by their parents' divorce or separation. Several mentioned that having a substance-abusing parent caused problems for them. Others had a hard time finding friends and getting acclimated to the school environment. A few students lost a parent to death during elementary school, middle school, or high school. Some students did not want to elaborate on their problems, answering "no comment." Others said that they had family problems that they did not care to discuss.

The following narratives are being provided in order to give educators a glimpse into the lives of students whose backgrounds may differ from their own and thereby make it easier for them to understand the behavior and schooling needs of students who come from challenging backgrounds. The case studies also underscore the strong impact of early schooling experiences on subsequent school years. Therefore, as noted in the Introduction, the narratives describe both the elementary and secondary schooling experiences of students to show how patterns begun in elementary school may or may not affect subsequent schooling experiences. All the students' names have been changed to protect their identity.

DESTINY

Destiny, a half-Black and half-Mexican high school senior, exuded confidence on the day when she was interviewed. She was attractive and knew it, and she had plenty to share regarding her schooling experiences. Unlike most of the students who were interviewed, she had attended elementary school and part of middle school in Louisiana, but her experiences there had a strong impact on her subsequent schooling experiences.

During first grade, Destiny's parents separated. This caused her to miss a lot of school. To compound things, because she was biracial, she was picked on by other kids at school, on the way to school, and after school. "I was picked on daily," Destiny said.

Because she was a good reader and enjoyed reading informational books, Destiny read during her spare time. She had books and magazines at home and sometimes used the public library. The school library, however, was off limits to her. "The librarians were mean," she said. "They were only nice to the White students."

As if her parents' separation, feeling unwelcome in the school library, and the daily harassment that she experienced from other children weren't enough, another incident occurred during elementary school that affected her schooling: A boy died at school one day, and Destiny's brother witnessed the tragedy. From that point on, Destiny was fearful of walking around the school. She became preoccupied with the death of this child and her brother's eyewitness account. As a result, she said, "I couldn't stay focused in class and nobody was trying to help me focus. I couldn't focus because I was being picked on and because of the death of this boy that my brother witnessed."

At some point, Destiny began to feel that certain elementary teachers did not care about her. She noticed that some kids were treated better because they were considered "smart" and others were not treated well because they were considered "dumb." She was placed in the "dumb" category. Destiny said, "From the way they treated me and the way they talked to me, I felt that they didn't care, so it was like out of school I was smart, but in school I didn't really apply myself to what I should."

The problems continued when Destiny started middle school. She experienced both academic and family problems. Moreover, in California, as in Louisiana, she was harassed by students who resented that she was not "all Black" or "all Mexican." She said "I was picked on 'cause I caught the city bus and when we had just moved out here, I had on blue contacts and I was light skinned and I had long hair and long nails." At home, her mother tried to comfort Destiny and shared examples of discrimination that she herself had experienced.

When she arrived in California, Destiny also realized that she was behind academically. "When I moved out here, I wasn't where the other middle school students were. The teachers would tell us stuff that we should already know and I didn't know." Although Destiny knew that she was lacking information that the other middle school students had learned in elementary school, her teachers assumed that she was working below her potential in school. "They would shoo you away 'cause you're not trying and they didn't want to waste their time," she said. "I understood why they would feel that way." Destiny concluded that her middle school teachers did not care about her and that they thought that she would become a failure in life. She said, "I don't remember any of my middle school teachers that I got along with." One teacher told her that she would never graduate. According to Destiny, this teacher "didn't like me. He told me it was something I did in my elementary years that made me a bad child or something."

In high school, Destiny continued to have conflicts with other students who disliked her for being biracial. She was suspended from school three times for fighting or arguing. Her grades had improved, but at the time when she was interviewed, she was still behind academically. She failed a ninth grade English course, half of her tenth grade courses, and an English and math course during her senior year. Although she said that most of her high school teachers were good teachers, falling behind in elementary school (which consequently affected her middle school grades) was the reason why she was lacking credits during twelfth grade.

Destiny also noticed that the quality of instruction that she received varied according to the school that she attended. She had attended two high schools in the same school district and had vastly different experiences. She reported:

> I went to_____ high school and that was the worst experience of my life. That school was like a community. The students talked to the teachers like they were outside on the playground. Students don't respect the teachers and the teachers didn't respect the students. They talked to each other like they were friends, and honestly, the education isn't that good either because I didn't even try and I still made a 3.8 gpa. I can honestly say that I did not try at that school. The teachers know that the students don't do anything but they'll still slide them on by.
>
> I was attacked in my sixth period class by some Black girls who did not like me and the teacher ran out the classroom and let them fight me until the security guards came. I just do not like that school.

Even though Destiny's parents, a counselor, and some of her high school teachers had encouraged her to go to college, no one told her how to apply for college. Despite the fact that she was unsure of whether or not the school district had adequately prepared her for college, at the time of her interview, she was hoping to get admitted to a college or to attend a Fashion Institute. "I want to continue school," she said. "I want a higher education, and I want a high paying job. I think that going to college should be a good experience."

Whereas Destiny felt a lack of support from most of her elementary and middle school teachers, another student, Lorraine, credited her elementary teachers with providing her with the support that was lacking at home.

LORRAINE

At the time when Lorraine was interviewed, she planned to enlist in the Air Force and to attend college later. She was studying for the military entrance exam and had already spoken to a recruiter. Lorraine's father did not live with her during her childhood, but nevertheless she wanted to follow in his footsteps by joining the Air Force and then pursue sign language, business, or music as a career. Her enthusiasm about participating in the interview phase of the study was obvious and she seemed to be more mature than many high school seniors. Most people might be shocked to learn that her mother was a drug addict and that her childhood and adolescence were filled with family problems. Lorraine's mother had moved to California from a rural area of Oklahoma, and Lorraine believed that naiveté about California's faster lifestyle was the reason her mother got hooked on drugs. Regarding her mother's addiction, she explained:

> She didn't know that I knew, but I knew. I was five or six. I don't know how I found out, but I knew my mother was doing drugs. I was little and it's weird. She had a pipe in her hand in the bathroom. She thought I didn't know what it was. I said, "What's that for?" She said, "Oh, nothing. I'm just going to clean the bathroom." Right then, I knew what it was. I think I had seen it on t.v.
>
> I tell people, "If you're doing drugs and you think your child doesn't know you're doing drugs, they do. They won't say anything to you because they don't want you to be embarrassed." I didn't want my mom to be embarrassed, so I didn't let her know that I knew, but I knew.

Although her mother was a drug addict, Lorraine received emotional support and encouragement from several individuals. Lorraine said, "My mom was a substance abuser but that didn't stop me, because I knew she had problems. But I needed to be strong for both of us. Usually, the kids whose mothers are substance abusers, they lack in school."

Because she had attended schools in the same district as many of her relatives, some of her elementary teachers knew her family well. These teachers, particularly her second, fifth, and sixth grade teachers—a White woman and two African American teachers—convinced Lorraine that they cared about her and wanted her to succeed in life. "I learned a lot from them," she said. "They taught my uncle, sister, brother, nephews, and me. They treated me like I was their child and you could tell that they had a passion for teaching." As a result of the strong impact that her elementary teachers, particularly the three aforementioned teachers, had on her, Lorraine used their characteristics as a measuring stick for other teachers. She explained, "If you are a good teacher, you have a passion for teaching. I can tell the difference when I walk in a classroom. I can tell if they really like teaching or not. Teachers that have passion don't give up. They want to look into things more if you have a problem. They're like, 'What's wrong? What's really wrong at home?' That's what they're worried about."

During elementary school, Lorraine's teachers and her older brother also started talking to her about college. Lorraine was certain that her teachers believed that she would become a successful adult. "They could see it," she stated. "They could really see it. It's very important to have family or someone who cares, someone else you can go to and talk about problems." Moreover, an aunt, who was an avid reader, modeled the importance of reading to her by constantly reading herself and by also reading to Lorraine. "She had a book club for adults," Lorraine said. A friend also bought Lorraine a subscription to *Highlights*, a popular children's magazine, and Lorraine became a good reader. "*Highlights* was the only thing that I really loved," she stated.

Aside from her family problems, the only negative memory that Lorraine remembered from her elementary school years was when she was suspended from school for fighting during fifth grade. Many years later, however, her recollections of elementary school were still overwhelmingly positive. "Right now, I still go and visit my elementary teachers," she said, proudly. She was thrilled that she was serving as an after-school volunteer at her former elementary school and was able to see her favorite teachers regularly.

Lorraine also had positive memories of her middle school years, even though she continued to have family problems. She felt that most of her teachers were good teachers who did an adequate job of preparing her for high school. Lorraine said, "My best middle school teacher Mrs. Shaw was my English teacher in seventh grade. She was dedicated. She loved her students and no one ever was bad in her class. She just loved her students."

By the time Lorraine was in high school, her mother had stopped using illegal drugs. The turning point for her mother came when she and Lorraine were nearly homeless. "We were living with other people," Lorraine recounted, "and we were going to have to sleep on the ground. I heard my mother say, 'I can't do this anymore.'"

Although her mother stopped using drugs, Lorraine said that she continued to have "family problems." "There were times when I wasn't into school," she said. Most of her classes were college preparatory courses, and she had one honors class. In ninth grade, Lorraine failed an algebra class. "I thought I was doing good, but really, I couldn't handle it," she stated.

Overall, however, Lorraine felt that her high school years were positive ones. She was a member of Student Council and planned assemblies and Homecoming. She gave a high rating to the quality of teaching and the quality of counseling about college that she received. Lorraine's "best" high school teacher taught a world geography class and an American history class that she took. "He was very patient and he likes teaching," she said. "He's fun and you learn a lot." In Lorraine's opinion, the school district had done "everything in their power to prepare us for college." Her one regret was that the school district did not make enough effort to reach her mother. She explained, "They need to get the parents more involved because my mom says that she wishes she had been more involved with me, like get lists of my homework assignments and making sure I really did them. The parents don't know what the kids are doing. Sometimes, I wouldn't do my homework and my mom didn't know."

BRIANA

Like Lorraine, Briana's childhood was affected by her mother's drug addiction. At the time when she was interviewed, seventeen-year-old Briana had already applied to a local four-year comprehensive university to major in business. "I'm like the first generation in my family to attend college," she said proudly, "and I want to attain that goal. I want to do it!" Briana described herself as "hardworking, outgoing, a role model to her four younger siblings, and a person who is willing to ask questions." She spoke candidly about her childhood.

> My mom was doing drugs, cocaine, pretty much for all of my education up until now. That could have had an effect on me but I didn't let it. She got hooked because of pressure. She had me when she was 14. A lot of her friends were smoking, drinking, partying. And she was young, a teen mom, and she did the same things that everybody else was doing. She dropped out of school at age 16 but got her GED later.
>
> I was about five years old and I remember my mom going out and not coming back for two days and me being in the house with all those kids, raising them. Sometimes she would leave at night and we wouldn't know she was gone until morning. Every time she'd leave, I'd call my grandma to come and get us. My grandma would take me to school.

Because of her mother's instability, Briana and her siblings were eventually taken in by relatives. Briana spent four years living with an aunt who had a foster care license, but later moved back in with her grandmother. "I was skipped around a lot," she said. "I lived with my grandma, then my aunt, and my grandma, and then my aunt, because I'm my grandma's baby. My grandma raised me and that's what I was used to. And with my aunt, it was different."

In spite of the hardships that Briana experienced in her personal life, at school she excelled. During third grade she was placed in the G.A.T.E. program. Although she rated the quality of instruction that she received in elementary school as "fair," she felt that most of her teachers cared about her and believed that she would become a successful adult. Her fondest memories center around her third grade teacher. Briana said, "She made personal stops to my house to make sure I was okay. If my real mom didn't pick me up, she would stay there with me until four o'clock or whatever time until somebody came and got me. And we talked during those times. We had a lot of quiet time together and a lot of personal time together. I think I was her special one."

The following year, however, Briana's relationship with her fourth grade teacher was not positive. "I never understood one word she said to me," Briana explained. "She called me by the wrong name. I'm sure nobody understood what she said. Whatever we were learning, we just caught on by hearsay." As a result, Briana's grandmother had her moved to another class.

Although she had some elementary teachers "who just could not connect with me, or I just could not connect with them," her overall impression of most of her elementary school teachers was positive. "I had teachers that went out of their way for me," she said. "They would tell me, 'You're going to be something in life. Keep doing what you're doing.' "

As a result of her hard work and outstanding achievement in elementary school, Briana was accepted to a prestigious preparatory middle school. The school was public, competitive, and prided itself on its selectivity and extremely high standardized test scores. Moreover, because she had started school early, Briana was only ten years old when she entered the school. "I knew what was expected the day I went in there," she said. "It was tough."

During this time, Briana was living with her mother again. "That's when she started going on her escapades for three or four nights in a row," Briana said. Nevertheless, Briana made sure that her younger sisters and brother caught the bus to school, and then she caught a bus herself to school. She refused to let her mother's problems affect her schooling. Briana's attitude was "I'm not going to do what my mom did," she stated, and "I refused to use her as an excuse for my problems." Briana's resilient outlook and the strong support that she received at the preparatory school contributed to her success in middle school. She kept her grades up and did not fail any courses. "They won't let you fail," she stated, "because if you fail, you can't go on over there. You have to be on a point system and if you fail, you're on probation and you don't get to do anything. You don't want to fail."

Whereas Briana rated the quality of her elementary school instruction as "fair," she rated that of middle school as "excellent." "It was just a different realm," she stated. Despite the fact that she had a negative experience with her seventh grade math teacher, whom she suspected of being racist, Briana thought that most of her middle school teachers cared about her personally, believed that she would eventually graduate from high school, and believed that she would become a successful adult. She stated, "I had the best teachers there. Wow! They were so good. They taught me things I just knew were worth something. I still use that information now. I had teachers go out of their way for me, to help me get what they were talking about. They always went out of their way."

Although Briana had a favorable impression of most of her middle school teachers, her "best" teacher was her seventh grade English teacher, an African American woman who had high expectations. Briana explained, "She gave us so many hands on activities and I love hands on activities. It made you understand. I remember the first day of school, I got in trouble because I had the worst handwriting in the classroom and she said, 'I'm not dealing with this. I'm going to give you a packet and you're going to do it.' And now my handwriting is so much better. She was my first Black teacher. She was remarkable. I liked her."

In high school, Briana's attitude about school changed. She felt both academic and social pressures. The academic pressures resulted in her failing a class, a ninth grade English course, for her first and only time. "I guess, I was just being lazy," she stated. The social pressures, however, resulted in her decision to leave the honors program at the end of ninth grade. Briana explained, "I was the only Black person in almost every single one of my classes. I knew Black people from my elementary school, and I wanted to mix in with other people because I felt stupid. I was in classes with all of these Caucasians. The way they talk and everything was just so different. I understood what they were saying but I wanted to mix in. I wanted to move and get out, because I don't like honors classes."

As a result, she was placed in college preparatory classes, which are less rigorous and less selective than G.A.T.E., honors, and advanced placement courses. She felt more comfortable and had classes that had more African American students in them. Moreover, she felt that the college preparatory teachers were just as good as the honors teachers. Briana also believed that most of her college preparatory teachers believed that she would become successful. Her best high school teacher, however, was a Latino who taught eleventh and twelfth grade English. "He goes out of his way for me and I love his teaching," she said. "He connects with us. He talks to us at our level."

At the time of Briana's interview, her mother had recently gotten off of drugs. Briana credited her siblings and herself with her mother's lifestyle change. "When she was on drugs, we didn't really express ourselves to her because we were young. As we got older, we told her how we felt and how it was affecting us," Briana stated. Nevertheless, Briana had decided to stay with her grandmother, instead of moving to another city to live with her mother. She did not want to uproot herself during senior year, because she was already acclimated to the school and too close to graduation.

SUMMARY

It is evident from the three narratives in this chapter that the elementary school experiences are precursors of future schooling experiences. They set the tone, either positively or negatively, for subsequent schooling experiences. Destiny's early negative schooling experiences affected her academic development and appeared to foreshadow the remainder of her years in school. Because she fell behind academically during elementary school, she remained behind during middle school and high school. As a result, she was still struggling to catch up, during her senior year.

Conversely, Lorraine's and Briana's elementary schooling experiences were mostly positive. They felt that their teachers cared about them and that their teachers believed that they would become successful adults. Lorraine even continued to have a positive relationship with some of her elementary teachers many years later. Unlike Destiny, Lorraine and Briana also had positive memories of their middle school and high school years. Whereas Destiny had failed courses in middle school and high school, both Lorraine and Briana had failed one course and that was in high school. During middle school, Destiny was given the impression that she was not "college material." Lorraine, on the other hand, felt that her teachers had done an adequate job of preparing her for college, and when she was quite young, teachers and her older brother began to plant a seed in her mind about attending college. Because of her outstanding performance in elementary school, Briana was chosen to attend a prestigious college preparatory middle school. Everyone, including her drug-abusing mother, expected her to eventually attend college.

One of the strongest messages that the narratives contain is that school can either exacerbate or ameliorate other stressors in children's lives. All of the girls who were profiled in this chapter came from problematic homes. Destiny's parents' separation had an adverse effect on her, and she experienced hostility from individuals who could not accept her biracialism. She also was deeply affected by the death of a schoolmate. Lorraine's mother and Briana's mother were drug addicts. The most apparent difference that surfaced among the narratives is that Lorraine had support from elementary school teachers, an older brother, and an aunt. Briana had support from her grandmother, aunt, and teachers. Although Destiny mentioned having received support from her mother, she felt that her teachers viewed her negatively early on. As a result, "Out of school, I was smart," she said, "but in school I didn't really apply myself." Cummins's (1986) assertion that minority students are "empowered" or "disabled" as a result of their interactions with educators appears to be borne out by the experiences of the students who were portrayed in this chapter.

A second message from the narratives is that because of their own problems and personal issues, some parents are ill equipped to provide the academic support that their children may need. In such cases, other family members may be able to compensate. In cases where there is no other family member to take up the slack, teachers can be doubly influential (Thompson, 1998b). The teachers who went out of their way to take a personal interest in the students were greatly appreciated by the teens whose narratives were presented in this chapter.

Another strong message is that children should be neither judged nor penalized because of their home environments; nor should they be expected to follow in the negative footsteps of a parent or another family member. Even though two of the teens were exposed to their mothers' constant drug abuse, each was resilient and determined not to follow the same path. Moreover, both teens chose to use education to improve the quality of their lives. Furthermore, they did not perceive themselves to be victims. They accepted the realities of their home lives and accepted responsibility for their own future. Their resiliency and strong desire for a better future permeated their narratives.

The narratives also illustrate that although elementary educators can do little to change children's home lives, educators can do much to change the quality of children's future and outlook on life by (1) convincing them that they can succeed in life; (2) providing positive role models in the form of caring teachers, counselors, and administrators; (3) equipping students with the tools that they will need to excel in middle school; (4) providing a safe haven in the form of welcoming, nurturing, and structured classroom environments; (5) giving them a positive viewpoint of school through positive initial schooling experiences; and (6) not disparaging their home lives. Both Briana and Lorraine clearly loved their mothers. Although they spoke of their mothers' behaviors in a straightforward manner, they never spoke of their mothers disparagingly.

A final message that surfaced from the narratives concerns tracking. Briana's high academic achievement resulted in her being accepted into the G.A.T.E. program in elementary school and a prestigious college preparatory middle school. In high school, however, she was upset that she was the only African American student in most of her classes. She felt ostracized and wanted to mix with other Black students. Therefore, she voluntarily left the G.A.T.E. program.

The fact that she was the only African American in most of her honors classes indicates that tracking was probably widespread in her school district. Although she could handle the academic workload, she could not handle being an outsider among students who came from mainstream culture. Fordham's theory (1988) states that in order to become successful by American standards, African American students are forced to reject the ethos of their native communities (fictive kinship) and adopt the ethos, which is individual centered, of the dominant culture. As a result, these students downplay their race. Comer and Poussaint (1992) said that stereotypes about race that result in certain students being accused of not being "black enough" or of "acting white" can be extremely detrimental to African American students. Delpit (1995) found that there is a "culture of power" in America, from which many minority students are being excluded, because educators are not teaching these students about it. As a result, these minority students are unaware of certain rules and skills that they need to know and possess in order to compete academically.

In Briana's case, being different from students from mainstream culture increased her sense of social isolation in her honors classes. Her experiences underscore the fact that tracking hurts two groups: those who have historically been excluded from higher-level academic tracks and those students from nonmainstream backgrounds who find themselves as the "chosen" few. In order to lessen these problems, educators must broaden their perspectives regarding who should be "chosen" and who should be excluded. A broader perspective would result in more African American children being placed in higher-level tracks. Consequently, a "critical mass" of African American G.A.T.E. students would decrease the sense of social and cultural isolation that students like Briana face. Other issues pertaining to tracking will be discussed in ensuing chapters.

2

Early Reading Habits and Attitudes about Reading

In African American culture, literacy has had a rocky history. During the slavery era, America went to great lengths to control, suppress, and eventually prohibit the instruction and education of slaves and free Blacks in the South (Fleming, 1976). Although some slaves still managed to learn to read and write during this period, by the advent of the Civil War, most Blacks were illiterate.

Today, it is well known that literacy and academic success are strongly correlated. Moreover, children who live in print-rich environments in which they have had lots of exposure to books and lots of opportunities to be read to, enter school with stronger literacy skills than others. Although reading is the foundation on which academic success rests (Chall, 1967; Flesch, 1955), African American children's reading scores, like their scores in other areas, are cause for alarm.

Gunning (2000) revealed that during fourth grade, reading demands increase and children are required to read texts that have more challenging vocabulary and concepts. Gillet and Temple (2000) said that the heavy reliance on nonfiction versus fiction texts plays a role in reading difficulties that begin to appear around fourth grade. Indrisano and Chall (1995) stated that differences between the reading skills of poor and middle-class children become apparent during fourth grade, and by middle school the poor children have fallen even further behind their middle-class peers. Honig (1999) cited numerous problems that poor readers in the upper elementary grades experience. Among them are poor motivation, a lack of confidence, poor spelling, weak vocabulary, and poor decoding skills.

Consequently, researchers have found that a disproportionate number of children from minority backgrounds have fallen behind by fourth grade (Au, 1993). Kunjufu (1985) described a phenomenon that he labeled "Fourth-Grade Failure Syndrome" that affects many African American boys. The National Assessment of Educational Progress (NAEP) indicated that there are substantial differences in the reading achievement levels of fourth graders along racial/ethnic lines. Whereas an estimated 39 percent of fourth graders who were tested in 1998 scored below the basic reading level, substantially higher percentages of African American, Hispanic, and Native American fourth graders did so (National Center for Education Statistics, 1999d). This is particularly troubling because researchers have found that children who are academically behind at the end of third grade tend to remain behind for the rest of their years in school (Queen, 1999). Alexander, Entwisle, and Dauber (1994) found that even when children who are performing below grade level are retained in a grade, they tend to remain behind their peers for the duration of their schooling and the benefits of retention appear to be temporary.

There are similar problems among secondary students. Disproportionately higher percentages of minority middle school and high school students continue to struggle with reading after leaving elementary school. According to NAEP, whereas an estimated 28 percent of the total sample of eighth graders in public schools nationwide scored below the basic reading level, only 19 percent of Whites did so. Conversely, 50 percent of Black and 48 percent of Hispanic eighth graders did so. Among high school seniors, 23 percent of the total sample of seniors, but only 17 percent of the White students, scored below the basic reading achievement level. Conversely, substantially higher percentages of Black (43 percent) and Hispanic (36 percent) seniors did so (National Center for Education Statistics,1999a).

Besides the obvious and well-known benefits of reading, another often overlooked advantage is the joy that stems from pleasure reading or the aesthetic side of reading (Cone,1996; Rosenblatt,1995). Another benefit of reading is that it can be used as a coping strategy. In today's postmodern world, stress has become a popular term. While exploring the links between rage and madness, Diamond (1996) remarked that one indicator of the high levels of stress that many Americans experience is the increasing level of violence in American society. Whereas some individuals resort to violence to deal with stress, others have found reading to be an effective strategy to help them cope with adversity. In an earlier study, Thompson (1999a), found that nearly 21 percent of the African Americans who participated in the study had relied on reading as a coping tool for adversity during childhood and or adolescence.

Krashen (1993) mentioned several African Americans, including Malcolm X, author Richard Wright, and neurosurgeon Ben Carson, who used reading as a coping strategy. Tardif and Sternberg (1988) found a link between reading and creativity. In their review of literature pertaining to creativity, they discovered that during childhood, creative adults felt more comfortable with books than with people. Destiny's narrative (see chapter 1) illustrates how one African American child used reading to cope with difficult circumstances.

In spite of all of the positive benefits of good reading skills, the public school system continues to grapple with ways to improve students' reading scores. Often, however, common school practices actually become barriers to literacy. Shannon (1992), for example, described how certain practices become deterrents to literacy. He found that some kindergarten teachers place children in reading groups according to their social skills, instead of academic aptitude. These children will most likely continue to be placed in such groups in succeeding grades. Children who are poor and members of ethnic minority groups are most likely to end up in low-level reading groups. Children in low-level reading groups usually receive the worst instruction and have the fewest opportunities to read. Interruptions by the teacher and classmates are common. Hale (1986) said that when African American children have poor reading scores, cognitive deficits are blamed. Conversely, when White middle-class children have poor reading scores, other factors are blamed.

One of the most blatant examples of a common school practice that serves as a deterrent to reading takes place at a predominantly Black elementary school in the region in which many of the participants in the current study reside. At this school, children are not permitted to check out books from the school library unless they are accompanied by a parent. Regardless of the reason for this practice, children in a region where poor reading skills and poverty are pervasive are being dissuaded from using the school library.

Reading is one of the most important determinants of academic success. Because disproportionately high numbers of African American students have weak reading skills, feedback from African American students regarding their early reading habits and attitudes can be extremely beneficial to educators and policymakers. Students who participated in the interview phase of the study were asked ten questions about their early reading habits and attitudes about reading. The results are presented in this chapter. Two narratives, one of a struggling reader and one of a good reader, follow. As with other narratives, both elementary and secondary schooling experiences are described.

EARLY READING HABITS, SKILLS, AND ATTITUDES

Eighty-two percent of the students who participated in the interview phase of the study said that they were good readers when they were in elementary school, but only 57 percent said that they had actually enjoyed reading when they were younger. Those who liked to read during elementary school tended to find it pleasurable because they were good at it, they learned a lot from reading, or they saw it modeled at home.

One student said that she liked to read during elementary school because reading "builds vocabulary. Books are my friends and I get to meet different people when I read." Another student said that she liked to read because she had more freedom to select books that interested her during elementary school. She explained, "In elementary you get to pick what kind of books you want to read. In high school you have to read what the teacher picks. If you don't like the book, you just have to deal with it. Very rarely will they let you choose your own book." A boy said that he loved to read because, "My parents always had a book. My parents would read while the t.v. was on." A G.A.T.E. student said, "I love to read. If I would read a story, it would take me away to another place."

Conversely, students who said that they disliked reading during elementary school, tended to dislike it because they felt that it was boring, they had poor reading skills, or they had negative experiences that were associated with reading. For example, a boy who was in basic classes during elementary school said that he did not like to read because, "I stuttered." A G.A.T.E. student said that she disliked reading because, "My parents' religion required that we constantly had to read. I saw it as punishment because I couldn't watch t.v. until I read." Another G.A.T.E. student said that reading "just never appealed to me. It just didn't really float my boat. I'd do it if I had to." A student who took basic classes said what many students said: "Most of the books just didn't catch my attention." The most telling explanation of why some students disliked reading came from one of the two students whose narratives are presented later in this chapter.

TIME DEVOTED TO READING

Seventy-nine percent of the interviewees said that they read during their spare time. Slightly more than half the students who read during their spare time said that they did so two or three times per week. Nearly 40 percent said that they read daily during their spare time. Some of the students who disliked reading read during their spare time, and some who liked to read did not read during their spare time. Students who read during their spare time were most likely to read mysteries, science fiction, informational books, comic books, or young adult books. Several students said that they preferred reading adult novels, such as Stephen King books, during childhood. For example, a G.A.T.E. student said that she enjoyed reading "scary stories and mysteries, like Stephen King books. My mom thought I was crazy. She said I was supposed to be reading *Babysitters' Club*."

OWNING BOOKS AND USING LIBRARIES

Eighty-two percent of the interviewees said that they owned their own children's books and/or magazines during childhood. Among those who did not have their own books, several said that there were adult novels at home that they read.

Sixty-four percent said that they used the school library in elementary school. The majority used the school library for book reports or class projects. Only 25 percent of the interviewees used the school library for personal pleasure. Those who did not use it stated a number of reasons. The main reason was the limited selection of books. One student said that the books were "old and out of date." Another said, "They didn't have a lot of good books." A few, however, said that they felt uncomfortable in the school library or they were unaware that it even existed. For example, a girl said, "I didn't even know what the library was." Other students said that they had no need to use the school library because they had enough books at home.

An equal percentage (64 percent) of the students said that they used the public library while they were elementary students. These students were also more likely to use the public library for school related purposes versus personal interest. A girl who did use it for personal reasons said that she preferred the public library over the school library because the public library had a much wider selection of books. Another student preferred the public library because she was able to use the computers there. One student belonged to a reading incentive program at a public library. Students who did not use the public library cited transportation problems or the fact that they owned enough of their own books, so they did not feel that it was necessary to use the public library.

FAMILY LITERACY

Two questions related to "family literacy." Eighty-two percent of the interviewees said that during the period when they were in elementary school, they had at least one family member who read on a regular basis at home. More than half of the students said that they saw their mothers reading on a regular basis, and 32 percent said that their fathers read a lot. Fourteen percent said that a sibling read frequently, and 14 percent also said that another relative read often. One boy said, "My mom reads a novel a day." Another student said, "My mom loves to read."

Seventy-one percent of the interviewees said that a family member read to them when they were in elementary school. For example, more than half said that their mothers read to them. Twenty-five percent said that their fathers read to them. Seven percent said that a sibling read to them. Eighteen percent said that another relative read to them.

THE IMPORTANCE OF GOOD READING SKILLS

When asked "In your opinion, how important are good reading skills in helping students to succeed academically?" 86 percent of the students said "very important." One boy explained, "You need to know how to read 'cause, there are students now that are in high school, struggling in the twelfth grade to read." The two narratives that follow describe the elementary and secondary schooling experiences of two interviewees, one with strong reading skills and one with poor reading skills.

Celeste

At the time when she was interviewed, Celeste, a soft spoken Resource Specialist Program (RSP) student, was hoping that she would be admitted to Grambling University in Louisiana. (RSP is designed to provide assistance to students with learning disabilities through the help of a teacher's aide and other resources. RSP students may be enrolled in regular classes, but the aide may come into the classroom to assist them.) She had already applied to four colleges. Three of them were historically Black colleges. She explained:

> I chose Black schools because I think I'd learn more about our heritage. Plus, on top of that, I think I'll learn more. I think if I don't understand—it's hard for me—they'll be willing to work with me. I don't want to be racist, but some of these white schools out here, they don't be trying to help Black people.
>
> I'm in RSP, but they're trying to get me out of there because I'm an overachiever. When I wanted to get help, I went to them and they were like, "Now Celeste. This is what you have to do." But it seemed like I wasn't getting no help at all. I needed help with work to get into college and with the classwork too. Sometimes, I'll ask my teachers. They'll get frustrated. They'll say, "Were you listening?" I mean, I'm coming to you, 'cause evidently, I didn't understand.

Celeste's exasperation with her teachers had a long history that started in elementary school. She struggled with her school work and was eventually placed in the RSP program. The main problem was that words appeared blurred or backwards to her. This resulted in both academic and social problems for her. Celeste explained, "I got teased by students a lot in the classroom and outside. The teachers would just tell them to be quiet but the problem would still occur. This was throughout the whole time I was in RSP."

Celeste rated the quality of instruction that most of her elementary teachers provided as "poor." "Some took the time out to care about the students," she stated, "but most of them were there for a paycheck. They really didn't want to be there." Celeste's main criticism of her elementary teachers, however, stemmed from the fact that they failed to teach her how to read. "I think my reading could have been better if we'd had phonics in classes," she stated.

Although she gave a "poor" rating to the quality of instruction that she received in elementary school, and did not believe that most of her elementary teachers cared about her, Celeste did believe that most of them liked her, " 'Cause I was willing to work," she said. Conversely, she felt that most of her elementary teachers did not believe that she would eventually go to college or become a successful adult. "I couldn't read," she explained. "I couldn't do basic math. Some kids with a disability just drop out of school after ninth grade."

Even though she struggled with her school work for all of her elementary years, Celeste was not officially diagnosed as "dyslexic" until sixth grade. Prior to that time, in order to compensate for her poor reading skills, Celeste relied on an intricate system that involved the school, her mother, and her classmates. As a result, she became overly dependent on others. She stated:

> I was always depending on somebody to help me, like my RSP teachers or my mom. I would give her the book and ask her to do the work for me or just read it to me and then explain it and give me the answers because I thought I couldn't do it.
> In fifth grade, a teacher forced me to read and I felt bad. I was trying to read and kids were laughing at me. So I just got up and left. My house was right down the street, so I just got up and went home and just stayed there. I got in trouble by my mom. When I told her, she understood.

Moreover, once Celeste was placed in the RSP program, her chances of being retained in the same grade decreased. "When you are RSP," she said, "they always pass you to your right grade level. Basically, you don't be learning nothing, but you always pass. Even though you know you're failing, you always pass the class." Another strategy that Celeste used was copying her friends' homework.

During sixth grade, things changed somewhat for Celeste. After her teacher identified the cause of her academic problems, Celeste was officially diagnosed as "dyslexic." In her opinion, this teacher was the "best" of all her elementary teachers. Celeste explained, "No one noticed that I had it, just him. I thought I was stupid and I didn't know why. I just felt like I was stupid 'cause my brothers and my sisters made straight A's all the way through high school. I just felt like I was the dumbest one in the family. I mean, I got laughed at by my cousins and everybody."

Celeste's sixth grade teacher encouraged her mother to take her to a hospital that was known for testing children who had learning disabilities. The hospital also provided some assistance by demonstrating strategies to compensate for her dyslexia. The strategies were helpful to Celeste, but she continued to struggle with her school work.

During middle school, Celeste was acutely aware that she was lacking skills and information that she had missed during elementary school. "I was still copying other people's work to get by," she admitted. She rated the quality of instruction that most of her middle school teachers provided as "poor." One eighth grade teacher tried to encourage Celeste. "She is the one who stuck with me and always told me that I could do it. She told me not to worry about other people laughing at me and stuff, and she was trying to help me read," Celeste said. Although she felt that most of her middle school teachers cared about her and liked her, she felt that they did not believe that she would become a successful adult or graduate from high school. Celeste said:

> They thought that I couldn't accomplish nothing. They always told my mom, "Why don't you just put her in a Special Day Class, where she leaves early, because we don't think she's going to graduate?" My mom always told me I could do anything. Sometimes, I felt like dropping out of high school, middle school, and elementary, but didn't, 'cause I don't wanna be stupider. Sometimes, I still feel stupid, 'cause for so many years I felt that way.

For Celeste, the first two years of high school followed the pattern of her elementary and middle school years. She failed two classes, copied other students' work, and relied on avoidance techniques. She explained, "In ninth and tenth grade, I didn't know how to read at all. I'd just go to class, open a book and go to sleep, so teachers wouldn't call on me. If a teacher tried to force me to read, I would just sit there and look at them. Then they would give me a Referral to the office."

In an effort to build her confidence and sight vocabulary, one ninth-grade English teacher gave Celeste "baby" books to read. At the end of tenth grade, Celeste finally got the help that she needed, when an RSP teacher began to teach her how to decode words. "She was the only RSP teacher that took the time," Celeste stated. "Learning phonics made a big difference for me. I stopped copying when I learned how to read and when teachers would explain a little. I felt good when I didn't have to copy other people."

Learning phonics increased Celeste's confidence about reading, and she proudly demonstrated her reading skills during the interview by reading a challenging passage of text fluently. Although her junior and senior years of high school were much better than her previous years of school, she did not believe that the school district had adequately prepared her for college. "I don't think I'm prepared to go to a university," she admitted. "Some of the kids feel the same way as me, because it's like some of the work that teachers give you is easy baby work. I still don't know how to write an essay yet." Despite this candid admission, Celeste was still hopeful that she would eventually be admitted into one of the colleges, particularly a historically Black college, to which she had applied.

Marcel

At the time of his interview, Marcel, another African American high school senior, was planning to go into the Navy after graduation. Later, he planned to attend Florida State University or Oregon State University to major in science. Unlike Celeste, Marcel, a senior who attended the same high school as Celeste, gave high ratings to the quality of instruction provided by his elementary, middle school, and high school teachers.

Marcel had positive memories of his elementary school years. He felt that his teachers were excellent, they cared about him, liked him, and felt that he would graduate from high school and become a successful adult. In fact, starting in first grade and continuing through middle school and high school, teachers encouraged Marcel to go to college. He stated, "They could understand me and they would talk to me. They made me feel better about myself a lot of times and I appreciate them for that. I got in trouble a lot. I guess it was my temper. I had a real bad temper when I was younger because I would act bold. I could actually talk to them. It was like having another family at school. They treated us like we were their kids."

At home, Marcel's parents encouraged him to read, and they read to him on a regular basis. As a result, he developed strong reading skills and found reading enjoyable. According to Marcel, "Actually, my dad got me started with novels when I was in elementary school. He had me read *Malcolm X*, and *Roots*. Those are the two main books that I read but other than that I was reading books about King Arthur and Merlin, or something imaginary."

Marcel also participated in a university-sponsored reading enrichment program. "When you open a book, especially if you're a little kid," he stated, it's like a whole new world. Some stories catch you and you could see yourself actually doing something like that. You get excited sometimes." He also used the school and public libraries for book reports and projects. "Good reading skills are very important," Marcel said. "The way I see it, the better you're able to read, the better you'll be able to understand things."

Although he had positive memories of elementary school, Marcel experienced several obstacles during middle school. He explained, "I had a lot of problems and a lot of enemies there. It affected me, because I would go to class angry. This guy would mess with me part of the day and it would stick in my mind, so that I couldn't concentrate in class. I would be so mad and it just left me frustrated. I tried to do my work but I couldn't think of doing anything else but hurting that person."

Marcel rated the quality of instruction that most of his middle school teachers provided as "good." He did, however, fail his seventh and eighth grade math courses and felt that one teacher, who taught science, singled him out unfairly. "I couldn't stay interested in my work," he explained. "I'd go to class and when I was doing my work everybody else was talking. The next thing you know, her whole focus was my way, saying 'I know you started this whole conversation in this class.'"

In high school, Marcel was placed in college preparatory classes. He rated the quality of instruction that most of his teachers provided as "good," but said, "They could get us going, but they couldn't keep us. All of the work was boring." Marcel failed four high school courses—two foreign language and two math courses. Nevertheless, he accepted full responsibility. He stated, "It took a long time for me to mature a lot. I was making my own mistakes. If I wanted to, I could've done this and If I wanted to, I could've done that. But at times, I was so immature that I just didn't want to. I just wanted to go out, have a good time, and have fun."

Marcel believed that most of his high school teachers cared about him, liked him, and believed that he would graduate and become a successful adult. He explained, "They don't want us to come back for another year. They all want to see us up on that walkway and hand us our diplomas. I believe that there is nothing that would make any of the teachers here happier than to see us walk. We got some great teachers in our school. They really do care."

SUMMARY

This chapter presented several details pertaining to reading and African American students. The narratives described the elementary and secondary schooling experiences of two interviewees—a poor reader and a good reader. The overwhelming majority of students who participated in the interview phase of the study said that during elementary school, they were good readers, they read during their spare time, they owned children's books and/or magazines, at least one family member modeled reading at home, and a family member read to them on a regular basis. Moreover, nearly 90 percent said that they believe that good reading skills are not only important but necessary for academic success.

Although the majority of students said that they were good readers during elementary school, a much smaller percentage of students said that they actually enjoyed reading when they were younger. Boredom appeared to be the most common reason some students did not enjoy reading. Additionally, despite the fact that a high percentage of students said that they utilized the school library during elementary school, the lack of a variety of books was cited numerous times as a reason students either did not use the library, or only utilized it for school assignments. A wide selection of multicultural books, specifically those that have African American main characters, might have alleviated this problem.

The two narratives that were presented in this chapter also yielded some interesting findings. Both Celeste and Marcel attended elementary and middle school in the same school district and even attended the same high school. Nevertheless, their schooling experiences and related attitudes were qualitatively different.

From the beginning, Celeste struggled with reading, yet her teachers seemed unaware of how they could help her. In fact, she was not officially diagnosed as dyslexic until sixth grade. The assertions of researchers that children who fall behind academically in third and fourth grade appeared to be exemplified by Celeste's schooling experience. At every level, she struggled academically and developed an elaborate system to survive. She overrelied on her mother, RSP teachers, and peers. Moreover, even though she could not read, she was promoted to the next grade year after year. In her opinion, early on, teachers gave up on her and did not hide the fact that they believed that she would not graduate from high school or become a successful adult. At the end of tenth grade, however, when a teacher taught her how to decode words, Celeste finally learned to read. Her self-image improved, as did her schooling experiences. Nevertheless, she still suffered as a result of her early reading difficulties, stating, "Sometimes, I still feel stupid 'cause for so many years I felt that way." Although she had applied to numerous colleges at the time of her interview, she admitted that she realized that she really had not been adequately prepared for college. As she noted, she had not even been taught how to write an essay despite the fact that it was already her senior year.

Unlike Celeste, Marcel, whose father motivated him to read during childhood, had a favorable impression of most of his schooling experiences and the quality of instruction that he received. His elementary teachers even treated him "like family," he said. Marcel admitted that he had a bad temper, was immature, and was apathetic toward his school work. He accepted full responsibility for failing courses, but also noted that some teachers could not keep the students interested and the course work and teaching were boring. Nevertheless, he felt that most of his teachers had done a good job.

In "Skills and Other Dilemmas," Delpit (1995) discussed the instructional practices that are most beneficial to African American students. She stressed that many instructional practices stemming from the whole-language philosophy are beneficial to African American students. Delpit insisted, however, that skill development is crucial to the academic success of African American students. Unfortunately, a furor that was politically motivated erupted as a result of her emphasis on the importance of skill development. Her work was criticized and disparaged by some educators. In the meantime, the reading, math, and science scores of African American children, like Celeste, continued to lag dismally behind that of their counterparts of other racial/ethnic groups.

Today, the controversy continues over which method of teaching children to read is best. There are anti-phonics advocates and there are anti–whole language advocates. The acrimony has affected both teachers and children. A study involving 117 California educators conducted by Thompson (2000) revealed several noteworthy points regarding how the debate over reading methods has affected educators. One finding was that the majority of the educators said that the debate had increased their uncertainty over how to teach children to read. More than half the educators said that they had not received adequate training to teach reading. These findings are startling because 70 percent of the educators had more than five years of teaching experience and most of their teaching had been done in public, inner-city schools. Because inner-city schools in California have disproportionately high numbers of teachers who have Emergency Teaching Permits (Quality Counts, 2000), there is a great likelihood that many more teachers are inadequately prepared to teach children how to read.

Celeste's schooling experiences were adversely affected by the fact that her elementary teachers were ill equipped not only to identify the source of her reading problems but also to provide the assistance that she needed. Her case is all the more serious in light of the high percentage of African American children nationwide who have poor reading skills. Conversely, Marcel had strong reading skills and reported having had positive elementary school experiences. He attributed any problems that he had at school to his own actions.

One of the clearest messages emanating from the narratives is that within the same school and school district, students may have markedly different experiences. The quality of instruction that they receive, the way in which they are treated by teachers, and their perspectives of their schooling experiences may differ. As a result, inequality of educational opportunity can occur.

3

Elementary Teachers

Of all the educators that students encounter during their years in school, primary school teachers are among the most influential. These teachers introduce children to their first taste of the formal school setting. They also administer tests that are supposedly designed to measure children's strengths and weaknesses. As noted earlier, crucial decisions about children's aptitude are made during this time, and children are sorted into low-, average-, or high-ability groups.

In *Star Teachers of Children in Poverty*, Haberman (1995) differentiated between successful teachers of children in poverty and teachers who quit or fail. Quitters or failures employ many unsuccessful, yet commonly used strategies. Star teachers, on the other hand, use many nontraditional and innovative practices that stem from the mind-set that all children can learn and that learning is its own reward. Among the characteristics of star teachers are (1) They have a proactive attitude about discipline; (2) they attempt to work collaboratively with parents and do not assume that poor parents are unconcerned about their children's education; (3) they accept responsibility for motivating students to learn; (4) they know students on a personal level; (5) they use their background knowledge about the communities in which students reside and students' talents and interests to make the curriculum relevant and interesting; and (6) they assign homework that is meant to be shared in class and that students can successfully complete without the assistance of parents. Unfortunately, Haberman concluded that less than 9 percent of the teachers who teach children in poverty could be labeled as star teachers.

Foster and Peele (1999), Delpit (1995), and Ladson-Billings (1994) identified numerous characteristics of teachers who are successful with African American students. Among the characteristics that Ladson-Billings cited were that teachers believe that all students can become successful, treat students fairly, develop relationships with them that are not limited to the classroom, see themselves as part of the community, create a community of learners in their classrooms, and help students make connections between what they already know and new information. These teachers practice culturally relevant teaching methods, which permit African American students to excel academically and still retain their African American culture. Culturally relevant teaching does not—as in the case of Briana who voluntarily chose to leave the G.A.T.E. program in order to find classmates with whom she could identify (in chapter 1)—force students to choose one or the other, academics or their own culture.

Foster and Peele examined the characteristics of teachers who are successful with African American male students. They found that these teachers refuse to give up on students—even those who appear to be resistant or apathetic—develop positive relationships with their students, treat students respectfully, believe that all students can learn, link the curriculum to students' lives, and seek to nurture and motivate students. Delpit (1995) identified some of the same characteristics as the other researchers but also included the use of "authoritativeness" and a "black communicative" teaching style.

The African American high school seniors who participated in the current study answered numerous questions about teachers. One question pertained to teachers in general. The rest focused on elementary, middle school, or high school teachers as separate groups. The answers are important because they reveal what African American students expect from their teachers, how misunderstandings between African American students and teachers can be prevented, and what teachers can do to improve their success rates and their relationships with African American students.

QUALITIES OF OUTSTANDING TEACHERS

The students were asked, "In your opinion, what are the most important qualities of outstanding elementary, middle school, and high school teachers?" The students were asked to circle all listed characteristics that applied. (The list was based on responses from participants in an earlier field test.) Fifteen characteristics were listed, and students could add other characteristics that were not listed.

There were seven characteristics that the majority of students deemed important. Seventy-four percent of the students circled "Explains

Things Well" and 74 percent circled "Makes the Course Work Interest-ing" as the most important characteristics of outstanding teachers. "Gives Extra Help" was the next most frequently cited characteristic, which was followed by "Patience." "Fairness," "Friendliness," and "Humor" were also circled by more than half the students. Fifty percent of the students said that an outstanding teacher "Challenges Students Academically." "Gives Lots of Homework" and "Strictness" were the least cited characteristics. Table 3-1 provides more information regard-ing the characteristics that were the most and least important to African American students. It also shows differences among students according to whether or not they were retained during elementary school and according to their elementary track.

Some differences did surface among groups. For example, a higher percentage of students who were retained during elementary school than others said that outstanding teachers are "intelligent" and "give lots of homework." Students who were in Special Education during elementary school were less likely than other groups to associate out-standing teaching with "academic challenge," "intelligence," "pa-tience," "fairness," "friendliness," and "enthusiasm."

TABLE 3-1
Qualities of Outstanding Educators (by % of Students, Elementary Retainees, and Elementary Track)

Quality	Total Sample	Retainees	Spec. Ed	Basic	G.A.T.E.
1. Explains Things Well	74	62	64	74	75
2. Makes the Course Work Interesting	74	73	64	74	75
3. Gives Extra Help	67	65	55	70	63
4. Patience	66	50	18	68	71
5. Fairness	62	58	36	67	52
6. Friendliness	58	46	36	62	50
7. Humor	57	50	46	59	52
8. Challenges Students Academically	50	54	18	50	59
9. Intelligence	49	58	27	51	50
10. Makes the Course Work Relevant	42	46	18	41	50
11. Enthusiasm	39	15	0	39	46
12. Niceness	38	35	18	45	20
13. Gives Rewards	33	31	36	35	27
14. Strictness	28	42	36	29	25
15. Gives Lots of Homework	13	19	9	15	7

N = 271

During the questionnaire phase of the study, the students wrote more comments about qualities of outstanding teachers than any other topic. Students who participated in the interview phase of the study also made many comments about teacher qualities. A peer counselor, who participated in the interview phase of the study, said "Teachers need better training." A girl, who belonged to her school's Culture Club, said "Schools need better teachers who really want to teach. We also need more African American teachers and teachers who keep it real and prepare us better for life." Another girl said, "Ninety percent of the teachers shouldn't be here. They're all old and they're impatient." A boy, who had attended high school in two separate school districts, said, "We need teachers who are here for more than their paycheck, who actually care." A girl said, "I think there has to be a relationship with each student. I know it's hard but that's one of the challenges of being a teacher." Another boy spoke at length about teachers, saying:

You know how they say all a teacher needs is a degree in literature, or English or math? It gots to be more than that. I think if a teacher really wanted, they would go through everything. I would go through communications or sociology. That way you could be able to deal with the students, because a lot of teachers who come here, especially the brand new teachers, they can't handle it. The kids will act a fool. They will run out of the classroom and not care.

It's like, it takes a teacher years just to develop a backbone. Substitutes should be trained a lot more and not be so soft. If the teachers had more credentials, I think the school system will be a lot better. Learning would be more fun for the teachers and the students because the teacher would actually be able to talk to the students and have a relationship with the students. We don't only want to be considered students, we want to actually be friends with the teacher. We don't just want to go to class and not conversate with the teachers. Everything would be a lot better and teaching would be a lot easier.

BEST ELEMENTARY SCHOOL TEACHERS

Thirty-three percent of the students said that they had more than one "best" elementary teacher. When asked to identify their "best" elementary school teacher(s), students' responses varied. No grade received even half of the students' votes. Forty-six percent of the students, however, said that they had their "best" elementary teacher in sixth grade, which was followed by 42 percent who picked fifth grade. First grade and kindergarten, respectively, were least likely to be identified as the grades when students had their "best" elementary school teachers. Table 3-2 provides more information about the students' responses to this question.

TABLE 3-2
Grades in Which Students Had Their Best Elementary Teachers

Grade	Percentage of Students
1. Sixth	46
2. Fifth	42
3. Fourth	40
4. Third	34
5. Second	32
6. Kindergarten	27
7. First	26

N = 271

Note: Because many students circled more than one answer, the percentage total exceeds 100.

Although several of the students who participated in the interview phase of the study could not remember having a "best" elementary school teacher, those who did gave vivid descriptions. The recurring theme was that the "best" teachers were teachers who took a personal interest in the students and appeared to care about them on a personal level.

A girl who had the same elementary teacher for two years said, "My fourth and fifth grade teacher was the best, because if you had trouble in class, she would call your parents immediately. She would really really try and she was pregnant too, during my fifth grade year." A boy said that his sixth grade teacher was the "best" because, "She always said that she loved you." One girl said that her second grade teacher was the "best" because "she was nice, made me want to learn, and tried to get my poems published." A boy who was on his high school basketball team said that both his fifth and sixth grade teachers were the "best" because "they bent over backwards to help." One boy said that his "best" elementary teacher taught sixth grade. "She was down to earth and you could talk to her about everything." A boy who ran track and was on the school's football team said that his fourth grade teacher "would tell you if you needed to work harder. She was one of those teachers who would call home, help you after school, and she made things fun for everybody." A boy who was the student representative on the local school board also selected his fourth grade teacher as the "best," mostly because of the teacher's encouragement at a time when this student had many family problems. He explained, "Mr. F. wasn't one of those teachers where you just did your work and left. He had a personal relationship. If you had a problem, he would try to see if he could help in any way. He wanted you to be in that class and he wanted you to succeed. Everyone loved him. Every year, he was the best teacher. Just this year, I saw him after six or seven years. It brought tears to my eyes."

WORST ELEMENTARY SCHOOL TEACHERS

Fourteen percent of the students said that they had more than one teacher who stood out as the "worst." Fifth grade teachers were most likely to be identified as the students' "worst" teachers, followed by fourth grade teachers. Kindergarten teachers were least likely to be identified as students' "worst" teachers. An equal percentage of students identified their third and sixth grade teachers as the "worst." In general, early elementary teachers versus upper elementary teachers were less likely to be labeled as the students' "worst" teachers. Table 3-3 provides more details about the students' responses to this question.

Several students who participated in the interview phase of the study said that they did not have a "worst" teacher or that they could not remember one. One girl said, "I never had any bad elementary teachers. Never! They start getting bad when you're older." Those who did, however, were quite vocal in recounting negative memories that were associated with these teachers.

One student said that his fourth grade teacher was the "worst" because "she was just mean to everybody. There was really nothing fun in her class. She wouldn't help. She'd give you the work, but she wouldn't help." A boy said that his second grade teacher was the "worst" because "she babied everybody. Some really bad things hap-

TABLE 3-3
Grades in Which Students Had Their Worst Elementary Teachers

Grade	Percentage of Students
1. Fifth	38
2. Fourth	28
3. Third	25
4. Sixth	25
5. Second	15
6. First	14
7. Kindergarten	7

N = 271

Note: Because many students circled more than one answer, percentage totals exceed 100.

pened to her because she wasn't assertive." Another student said that her fourth grade teacher was the "worst" because "she didn't like me and her class was boring." A girl who was on her high school track team said her third grade teacher was the "worst" because "she was impatient and she acted like she didn't want to be there." Another girl said that her first grade teacher "was mean." A football player said that his fifth grade teacher was "grouchy, didn't want to be there, and didn't want to teach." One girl said that her fourth grade teacher "didn't know how to teach. She always yelled at us. . . . She always threw things at us." Another girl said that her second grade teacher "had a bad mouth, called kids 'stupid,' and was mean." A boy said that his third grade teacher "wouldn't give extra help." A G.A.T.E. student said that his fifth grade teacher "didn't like me at all. I didn't understand the way he would teach and I'd ask lots of questions."

OTHER QUESTIONS PERTAINING TO ELEMENTARY SCHOOL TEACHERS

Students who were interviewed for the study answered additional questions about their elementary school teachers. The results follow.

Did Students Feel That Most of Their Elementary Teachers Liked Them?

Eighty-two percent of the interviewees said that they felt that the majority of their elementary school teachers had liked them personally. Seven percent felt that their elementary teachers disliked them and 11 percent said that they were unsure. All the students who felt that their teachers disliked them or who were uncertain of whether or not their teachers liked them were in basic classes during elementary school.

Did Students Feel That Their Elementary Teachers Cared about Them Personally?

When asked whether or not they thought that most of their elementary school teachers cared about them personally, 75 percent of the interviewees said that they did. A student who was placed in the G.A.T.E. program during elementary school explained, "I had personal relationships with at least four of my teachers in elementary school." A girl who played on her high school basketball team said that she knew that most of her elementary school teachers cared about her because she could talk to them. One boy said that he believed that most of his elementary teachers cared about him because "they could understand me. They would ask me what was wrong." A high school athlete who played football and ran track, said that he attended a predominantly Black elementary school. He felt that most of his teachers cared about him personally because "it was like a family thing. They didn't treat it like a job; they treated it like they wanted you to learn." Another student said, "They were always on my back making sure I did my work. They were there after school if I needed help. They were like another parent."

Conversely, the students who felt that most of their elementary teachers did not care about them tended to feel this way for similar reasons. With the exception of one G.A.T.E. student and one Special Education student, all the students who said that they did not feel that their elementary teachers cared about them were in basic classes. One student said that she did not believe that most of her elementary teachers cared about her because "only two actually called my house."

Did Students Think That Most of Their Elementary Teachers Believed That They Would Graduate from High School?

Eighty-six percent of the interviewees said they thought that their elementary teachers believed that they would graduate from high school one day. With the exception of one Special Education student and one G.A.T.E. student, those who felt differently were all in basic elementary classes. Surprisingly, several students who said that they believed that their elementary teachers cared about them personally said that most of those same teachers did not believe that they would graduate from high school or become successful adults.

Did Students Think That Most of Their Elementary Teachers Believed That They Would Become Successful Adults?

Seventy-five percent of the interviewees stated that most of their elementary teachers believed that they would become successful adults. With the exception of one G.A.T.E. and one Special Education student, those who felt otherwise were in basic elementary classes. A student who was one of the state's top track stars said, "They always talked about me running in the Olympics. They always wanted me to come back and visit but I haven't had a chance." She also knew that most of her elementary teachers thought that she would graduate from high school because "they actually encouraged me." Another student said that her teachers "would tell me 'You're going to be something in life.'" The two narratives that follow present different elementary and secondary schooling experiences from two African American males who attended different high schools in the same district.

FAISON

In comparison to many of the students who participated in the study, Faison, a half-Black and half-White teenager, came from a somewhat privileged background. Both his mother and stepfather were teachers, but Faison's childhood was not perfect. His parents divorced when he was in elementary school, and during high school, a member of his immediate family died. At the time of his interview, Faison had already been accepted to one of the two universities to which he had applied. He said that his parents started encouraging him to go to college when he was in preschool and starting in first grade, his elementary teachers also did so.

During elementary school, Faison was accepted into the G.A.T.E. program. He rated the quality of instruction that he received as "excellent" and said that most of his teachers liked him, cared about him, and believed that he would graduate and become a successful adult. Of all his elementary teachers, he considered his first grade teacher as the "best." In addition to being supportive of Faison while his parents were going through a divorce, this teacher, according to Faison, "cared about her students. More than anything, she always gave me a positive attitude and made me have a positive attitude," he said.

Faison did not mention his second grade teacher but stressed that his "worst" elementary teacher was his third and fifth grade teacher, a man whom he had for two years. "I was really a talkative kid," Faison stated. "This teacher would send me to other classes to do busy work. He was boring." Nevertheless, most of Faison's memories of elementary school were positive. Middle school, however, was different.

Whereas Faison rated the quality of instruction that he received in elementary school as "excellent," the quality of his middle school instruction was "between fair and poor." Faison was still in the G.A.T.E. program, but stated, "There was nothing really exciting about it. It was real repetitive." Ironically, Faison attended middle school in a more affluent school district than his elementary school district. Moreover, he did not believe that most of his middle school teachers cared about him and was unsure of whether or not they even liked him. Conversely, Faison was certain that most of his middle school teachers believed that he would eventually graduate from high school and become a successful adult. "I can't even remember the names of any of my middle school teachers," he said.

During high school, Faison attended three different schools, including a private school in another state. He rated the quality of instruction that he received in ninth grade as "fair," but did not believe that most of his ninth grade teachers cared about him. This high school is located in the same affluent area in which he attended middle school. The quality of instruction that he received in the out-of-state private school during tenth and eleventh grade, however, was "excellent," in his opinion. During his senior year, he returned to the same school district in which he had attended elementary school. He rated the quality of instruction that he received as "good." Faison felt that all of his high school teachers, including his ninth grade teachers, believed that he would graduate and become a successful adult. The fact that he never failed a course from elementary school through his senior year attests to one of the reasons why all of his teachers held this viewpoint of him.

RONALD

Like Faison, Ronald, another male interviewee, was also the son of an educator. At the time of his interview, he had applied to three colleges, because "you need it [education] to become successful," he stated. Unlike Faison, Ronald's elementary and middle school courses were basic instead of G.A.T.E. classes, and unlike Faison, most of his memories of elementary school were negative.

Ronald labeled himself as an "average" reader who did not enjoy reading during elementary school because the teachers required him to read "boring books." His mother read to him at home and he often saw her reading to herself; still Ronald stated, "If I didn't have to read, I wouldn't read."

As far as the quality of instruction that most of his elementary teachers provided, Ronald rated it as "poor." "It was slower than it is today," Ronald stated. "It wasn't as challenging as what kids get today." Moreover, Ronald felt that most of his elementary teachers did not care about him and felt that some even disliked him. "Teachers have their favorites," he said. Although Ronald stated that he did not have a personal relationship with most of his elementary teachers, he had vivid memories of many of them. He said,

> In first grade, I had a nice teacher. My second grade teacher liked me. My third grade teacher, she probably didn't like nobody. My fourth grade teacher didn't like me. I had a cousin in the class and we had problems because we talked a lot. We played games during class because we were bored. We didn't do the reading. You read a lot in fourth grade. We knew that she wouldn't call on us. She called on people she knew were good

readers. I noticed that she kept on choosing certain people, like girls—White girls.

The two elementary teachers who stood out in Ronald's mind the most were his fifth and sixth grade teachers. Ronald considered his fifth grade teacher to be his "best" and his sixth grade teacher to be his "worst" teacher. Concerning his fifth grade teacher, Ronald stated, "When he taught, he was fun. We could hold a conversation. He made the extra effort and got to know you and he still got everything taken care of."On the other hand, whereas fifth grade was a positive experience for Ronald, sixth grade was the opposite. For some reason, Ronald and his teacher did not get along. "We had a problem," he stated. "I felt like she didn't like me. She was always on my case, always on my case." By the end of the school year, the conflict had escalated. Ronald's mother decided to keep him at home for the last two weeks of school. "I didn't go to school," Ronald said. "I didn't go to the sixth grade graduation. I didn't go on the sixth grade field trip because my teacher had problems."

Ronald did not know whether or not most of his elementary teachers expected him to graduate from high school or become a successful adult. "We didn't really have a relationship," he explained. Years later, however, he learned that one teacher definitely expected him to fail. He stated,

> When I got older, my cousin told me what my third grade teacher had said about me behind my back sometimes. I guess I had made my cousin late coming in from recess. We didn't have the same class. I guess the teacher asked him why he was late and she said to him, "You need to change who you hang around with, because your cousin is no good." I guess she said something like, "You don't want to end up like your cousin." Recently, a girl who goes to school with me now told me the same thing.

In comparison to his elementary school experiences, overall, middle school was a more positive experience for Ronald. He rated the quality of instruction provided by most of his teachers as "good," explaining, "I learned a lot in math and social studies." Although he believed that most of his middle school teachers liked him, because they "gave compliments," he believed that only half of his teachers truly cared about him. Unlike his elementary teachers, Ronald felt that most of his middle school teachers expected him to eventually graduate from high school and to become a successful adult because they recognized that he had leadership qualities.

During high school, Ronald began to take college preparatory classes. He rated the quality of instruction as "good," because he learned a lot.

Moreover, he felt that most of his high school teachers cared about him, but attributed it to the fact that his mother had become an administrator in the school district. Ronald also felt that most of his high school teachers liked him, expected him to graduate from high school, and believed that he would become a successful adult. Although he had passed all his middle school courses, in high school he failed two courses—a foreign language class in ninth grade and a math class in eleventh grade. Ronald considered his ninth grade foreign language teacher to be his "worst" high school teacher. "He used to put me on the spot in class, make me make a fool out of myself, and then tell me to stay after class," Ronald said.

During middle school, Ronald's mother began to discuss college with him and some of his teachers did also. In high school, some of his teachers also spoke to him about college. Even though Ronald's mother was a school administrator within the same district in which he attended school, he said that his high school counselor never spoke to him of college. Despite this, Ronald was serious about attending college and was hopeful that he would begin the following September.

SUMMARY

The students who participated in the study described numerous memories pertaining to their elementary teachers. The overwhelming majority of students who were interviewed believed that most of their elementary school teachers liked them, cared about them, expected them to graduate from high school, and believed that they would become successful adults. Eighteen percent of the students did not believe that their elementary teachers liked them or were unsure whether they did or not. Twenty-five percent did not believe that their teachers cared about them personally or were uncertain about it. Fourteen percent either were unsure or did not believe that their elementary teachers expected them to graduate, and 25 percent didn't believe their teachers expected them to become successful adults.

About one third of the students who completed the survey said that they had more than one "best" teacher. Upper-elementary-level teachers were more likely than lower-elementary teachers to be cited as "best" teachers. Conversely, 14 percent of the students said that they had more than one "worst" teacher. Again, upper-elementary-grade teachers were also more likely than lower-level teachers to be cited as "worst" teachers. At least three explanations might account for these results.

One possibility is that upper-elementary-level teachers might have been more influential or might have made more of an impact—either positively or negatively—on students. The other possibility is that the students' recollections of their lower-elementary-level teachers may not have been as clear as that of teachers that they had later. A third explanation is more troubling. As noted earlier, researchers have found that third and fourth grade are pivotal years for African American children. Children who are performing below grade level at the end of third grade tend to remain academically behind for the rest of their years in school (Queen, 1999). Moreover, by fourth grade, disproportionately higher percentages of African American students have been tracked into Special Education programs. For this reason, a plausible explanation of why students were less likely to identify lower-level teachers as their "best" might be that students had more negative memories associated with the lower-elementary-school grades.

The results of the most important characteristics of outstanding elementary and secondary school teachers provide educators with invaluable feedback from African American students. Outstanding teachers, according to the students who completed the questionnaire, explain things well and make the course work interesting. Outstanding teachers also give extra help. They are patient, fair, friendly, and they are humorous. These teachers also challenge students academically. On the other hand, teachers who are not outstanding, fail to explain things well, do not make the course work interesting, and do not give extra help. These teachers are impatient, unfair, unfriendly, and do not inject humor into their instructional delivery. Moreover, their course work is too easy.

The feedback regarding the characteristics that African American students selected as most important reveal that although African American students value intelligence in their teachers, teachers' style of presentation, willingness to provide as much assistance as necessary, and their personalities and interpersonal skills appear to be more important. The students' responses imply that good teachers have good communication skills and are able to "explain things well." Good teachers also know how to make the course work interesting. They give extra help. They are fair, patient, and friendly. They also know how to inject humor into their instructional practices. More important: the characteristics that African American students deem most important cannot be or are not taught in most teacher education courses

There are correlations between the teacher characteristics that students deemed important and what researchers have found. Delpit (1995) discussed the importance of explicitness or direct instruction to the academic success of African American students, which might be another way of describing "explains things well," one of the two most frequently cited characteristics by the students in the current study. Ladson-Billings's (1994) findings that effective teachers of African American students believe that all students can become successful, treat students fairly, develop relationships with them that are not limited to the classroom, and help students make connections between what they already know and new information were reiterated by the students. Moreover, Foster and Peele's (1999) assertion that effective teachers of African American male students develop positive relationships with students and seek to nurture and motivate students was repeated numerous times during the interviews.

It is clear from the work of these researchers and the feedback from African American students that elementary teachers have the power to make lasting contributions to the personal and academic development of children. Furthermore, there is no magic formula. By merely studying the list of characteristics that students and researchers have identified and incorporating these characteristics into their personalities and method of instructional delivery, all elementary teachers can become successful with their African American students. It is evident from the feedback from students that many elementary school teachers are doing a wonderful job of providing their African American students with positive and meaningful schooling experiences. However, there are still many teachers who need attitude adjustments. Moreover, many students stated, during the interviews or by writing additional comments on the questionnaire, that some teachers need to be fired. These are teachers who, for whatever reason, do not like their African American students, do not care about them personally, do not believe that they will graduate from high school, and do not believe that they will become successful adults. These attitudes are dangerous and can become self-fulfilling prophecies. Therefore, the list of important teacher characteristics that has been provided in this chapter should be revisited frequently and used as a professional and personal growth assessment for all teachers who teach African American students.

4

Elementary Course Work and Homework

The course work that students receive in elementary school is ostensibly designed to provide them with the foundational skills and information that are needed for them to progress to the next grade. By the end of elementary school, students should have gained the prerequisite skills that are necessary for success in middle or junior high school.

Homework is usually perceived to be an extension of classwork. Homework can be used to prepare students for upcoming tests and can give them opportunities to reinforce skills and gain more practice in various areas. Eggen and Kauchauk (2001) stated that poorly designed course work and homework can actually have the opposite effect. Instead of aiding students' academic development, they can exacerbate students' frustration and can even become detrimental to students who have learning disabilities. When homework is used properly they noted, however, it can be extremely beneficial to students. Among the characteristics that Eggen and Kauchauk listed of an effective homework program are that the homework should be connected to course work and it should be graded.

Haberman (1995) said that traditional attitudes and practices about homework ensure failure for children who live in poverty. Often, teachers assign homework that the teachers themselves were unsuccessful in teaching during class time. Usually, parental assistance is required for successful completion of the homework, yet for a number of reasons, parents may be unable to assist their children with homework. As a result, teachers assume that the parents are unwilling to help. Conversely, according to Haberman, outstanding teachers of students from impoverished backgrounds assign relevant homework that is designed to be shared in class and that students can successfully complete on their own without parental assistance.

The questionnaire that was used for the current study contained questions about the students' course work, quality of instruction, and homework during elementary school. The African American students who participated in the interview phase of the study were given an opportunity to elaborate on each of these questions and to answer an additional question about course work.

IN WHICH GRADE(S) WAS THE COURSE WORK THE MOST DIFFICULT?

The students who completed the questionnaire were asked to identify the grade in which they had their "most difficult" course work. Students were most likely to say that an upper- versus lower-elementary-school grade was "most difficult" for them. Nearly 20 percent of the students, however, said that a lower elementary grade was the "most difficult" for them. Furthermore, 9 percent of the students said that at least two grades were equally the "most difficult." More than half the students identified grade six as the "most difficult" of all. There was a statistically significant correlation between the grade in which students had their "worst" teacher and the grade in which the course work was "most difficult" for them ($r = .29$; $p < .001$). Table 4-1 provides more information about the students' responses to this question.

TABLE 4-1
Grades in Which Students Had Their Most Difficult Elementary Course Work

Grade	Percentage of Students
1. Sixth	56
2. Fifth	39
3. Fourth	23
4. Third	9
5. Second	4
6. First	3
7. Kindergarten	3

N = 271

Note: Because many students circled more than one answer, the percentage total exceeds 100.

IN WHICH GRADE(S) WAS THE COURSE WORK EASIEST?

When asked to identify the elementary grade in which they had their "easiest" course work, students' responses yielded mixed results. Twenty-four percent of the students indicated that the course work in at least two of their elementary classes was equally as easy. Nevertheless, 63 percent said that the kindergarten curriculum was "easiest" for them, followed by 41 percent who selected the first grade curriculum. The percentages of students who chose second, third, fifth, and sixth grades were very similar. Conversely, students were least likely to say that their fourth grade course work was "easiest." Table 4-2 provides more information about students' responses to this question.

BENEFITS OF ELEMENTARY COURSE WORK

Students who participated in the interview phase of the study were also asked whether or not they thought that most of the course work that they did in their elementary classes was "beneficial." Sixty-one percent of the students said that their elementary course work was "beneficial." One student said that the course work "taught skills." Another student said that the course work "got you ready to go to the next level."

Conversely, 36 percent of the students said that the course work was "not beneficial" or it was only "somewhat beneficial." A G.A.T.E. student said, "The first three years was stuff I already knew." Another G.A.T.E. student said, "Maybe I wanted to be challenged more." Yet

TABLE 4-2
Grades in Which Students Had Their Easiest Elementary Course Work

Grade	Percentage of Students
1. Kindergarten	63
2. First	41
3. Third	33
4. Sixth	33
5. Second	32
6. Fifth	30
7. Fourth	24

N = 271

Note: Because many students circled more than one answer, the percentage total exceeds 100.

another G.A.T.E. student complained that the classes were too large, the curriculum was impersonal, and "I just wrote stuff on paper and just turned it in." A student who was in Basic classes during elementary school said, "I didn't really learn anything." Another student said that his math and science course work were "beneficial" but "everything else was a waste of time." Two other students who took basic classes said that the course work failed to prepare them for middle school.

THE QUALITY OF INSTRUCTION THAT ELEMENTARY TEACHERS PROVIDED

When asked to rate the quality of instruction that most of their elementary school teachers provided, most students who completed the questionnaire rated it as "good" or "excellent." A higher percentage of G.A.T.E. students gave it a high rating and a higher percentage of Special Education students than others gave it a lower rating. Additionally, those who repeated an elementary grade were less likely to give a high rating to the quality of instruction (see Table 4-3).

One student said that she rated the quality of instruction that she received in elementary school as "excellent" because the teachers cared. Another student said that she rated it as "excellent" because "I loved elementary school and I think that all of my teachers did a great job." A student said that she rated the overall quality of instruction as "good" because "I learned a lot and had some teachers twice." Another student rated the quality of instruction at his elementary school as "fair" because the teachers "just taught the lesson but they weren't worried about teaching." One student said that she rated it as "poor" because the instructional pace was too slow and the work was not challenging enough.

TABLE 4-3
How Students Rated the Overall Quality of Instruction Provided by Most of Their Elementary Teachers (by % of Students, Retainees, and Elementary Track)

Student Type	Poor	Fair	Good	Excellent
Total Sample	3	19	57	21
Retainees	8	19	58	15
Special Education	9	27	27	36
Basic	3	19	62	16
G.A.T.E.	2	16	48	34

N = 271

THE AMOUNT OF HOMEWORK THAT
ELEMENTARY TEACHERS ASSIGNED

The students who completed the questionnaire were asked how often they were given homework assignments by most of their elementary teachers. About half of the students said that they received homework on a daily basis and only 10 percent said that they received homework once or twice a week. A higher percentage of Special Education students and those who were retained during elementary school than others received homework once or twice a week. A higher percentage of G.A.T.E. students, however, received homework four or five times per week. Students were also likely to receive more homework during the upper- versus lower-elementary grades. Table 4-4 provides more information about the students' responses.

THE AMOUNT OF TIME THAT STUDENTS SPENT
ON THEIR ELEMENTARY SCHOOL HOMEWORK

The students who completed the questionnaire were also asked how much time they spent on homework during elementary school. The majority of students spent three hours or less on homework per week. Students who received more homework than others were more likely to spend more time on it. The time spent on homework varied according to students' academic track. The overwhelming majority of elementary Special Education students and students who were retained during elementary school spent one hour or less on homework per week. A higher percentage of G.A.T.E. versus other students spent four or more hours per week on homework (see Table 4-5). One student wrote on the questionnaire that teachers should

TABLE 4-4
The Number of Days per Week That Students Received Homework during Elementary School (by % of Students, Retainees, and Elementary Track)

Frequency per Week	One	Two	Three	Four	Daily
Total Sample	4	6	20	18	51
Retainees	19	4	8	15	54
Special Ed.	18	9	27	0	46
Basic	5	6	20	17	52
G.A.T.E.	0	4	18	25	48

N = 271

TABLE 4-5
The Number of Hours per Week That Students Spent on Homework
Assignments during Elementary School (by % of Students, Retainees, and Elementary Track)

Elem. Track	1 or less	2–3	4–5	6 or more
Total Sample	35	35	20	7
Retainees	65	15	12	4
Special Ed.	82	9	0	9
Basic	36	37	19	7
G.A.T.E.	27	36	27	9

N = 271

"give an appropriate amount of homework—a medium amount— daily." Another student made a similar comment by stating, "An outstanding teacher gives not a lot of homework, but daily homework."

BENEFITS OF ELEMENTARY SCHOOL HOMEWORK

The students who completed the questionnaire were also asked whether or not they thought that the homework was "beneficial." Forty-four percent of the students said that the homework was "beneficial." Of those who did, most felt that the homework taught them important skills. There was a statistically significant correlation between the grade when students had their "best" elementary school teacher and how they rated the benefits of their homework (r = .35; p < .001). Those who said that they had their "best" teacher in an upper elementary grade were more likely to say that the homework they received was "beneficial." Conversely, almost half the students said that their elementary school homework was only "somewhat beneficial." A higher percentage of elementary retainees and Special Education students said that the homework was "somewhat beneficial" or "not beneficial" at all. A higher percentage of G.A.T.E. students said that it was "beneficial" (see Table 4-6).

One student wrote on her questionnaire, "I don't think giving homework is important, but working more one-to-one with each student is." A student who took basic classes said that her elementary school teachers "gave a lot of homework but there was too much." Another student who took basic classes said, "I really didn't have homework." The two narratives that follow will provide additional information about the students' elementary schooling experiences and how they relate to subsequent schooling experiences.

TABLE 4-6

How Students Rated the Benefits of Their Elementary School Homework
(by % of Students, Retainees, and Their Elementary Track)

Elem. Track	Not Beneficial	Somewhat Beneficial	Beneficial
Total Sample	7	48	44
Retainees	12	65	19
Special Ed.	9	64	18
Basic	8	49	43
G.A.T.E.	5	41	54

N = 271

LAVETTE

At the time of her interview, Lavette, who was involved in journalism and her high school's Culture Club as extracurricular activities, had applied to a private university in Los Angeles. She had taken college preparatory classes and was hoping that a college education would improve her job opportunities in "a career that I like," and also provide her with financial stability.

During elementary school, Lavette attended a predominantly Black school in a school district that was different from her current district. She rated the quality of instruction that she received as "good" because she "learned a lot." She also believed that most of her elementary school teachers cared about her, liked her, and believed that she would graduate. A negative memory, however, concerned homework and the woman Lavette labeled as her "worst" teacher. Lavette explained, "I had my worst teacher in the first or second grade. She was mean, because if we didn't do our homework right, we used to have to stand under a curtain. We couldn't have recess. We had Time Out and we would do Standards if we talked in class. She was a mean lady. She was old too. She was real rude. I didn't like her." Another negative memory pertained to the death of one of Lavette's classmates. "One of my friends died," she recounted. "It was real sad for all of us. We went to her funeral and then, over time we just got over it. She was in one of my classes and I was in fifth or sixth grade."

Another of Lavette's elementary school experiences could have been perceived as a negative event. Instead, she viewed it as something that helped her. In third grade, Lavette was retained. She said that retention helped her "to get focused." Lavette also believed that most of the course work and homework that she received was helpful to her. She recollected,

The homework was really beneficial. I remember that I had trouble learning the multiplication tables. Every single day, I used to write them. By the end of the school year, I knew all my tables, one through twelve. We used to have all kinds of vocabulary words—words I never heard of before. When you're in high school, English is boring, but in elementary school, it's fun. We used to get a homework packet on Monday. It was due on Friday. Elementary seemed fun because the teachers are more into it and they spend more time with you. They encourage you. In high school, they talk too much. They want you to be quiet. They write Referrals for anything you do. If you talk back to them, you can get a Referral. And you'll get in trouble and get kicked out.

Because her family moved, Lavette attended junior high in two different school districts. "Changing schools and having to make new friends was difficult," she said. In eighth grade, Lavette failed a math class but still rated the quality of instruction provided by most of her teachers as "good." "They assigned interesting group work," she explained. Although Lavette believed that most of her junior high school teachers liked her because "they were nice to me," she did not believe that most of them truly cared about her. "They always told us, 'I don't care if you learn or not. I'm still getting paid,'" she stated. Moreover, Lavette was uncertain about whether or not most of her junior high school teachers expected her to graduate or believed that she would become a successful adult. "They didn't really talk to us about high school," she explained. "I used to always tell them that I was going to be successful but I don't know if they believed me or not."

During ninth and tenth grade, Lavette attended school in the same predominantly Black district where she attended elementary school. She failed a tenth grade math course, yet still considered the quality of instruction that she received as "excellent." Most of her teachers were Black, and Lavette believed that they cared about her, liked her, and expected her to graduate and to become a successful adult. She recounted,

> They were so nice. They used to give us lunch money and buy us stuff for our classes.
> They used to give us stuff if we did good. It was cool out there. It was real interesting. They used to always tell us like how we were minorities and how we should take education seriously and how our parents pay taxes—money for us to go to school. They would tell us how important education is and how Whites think less of us, how we should prove them wrong. They used to tell us that all Black people are not ignorant. Some Black people have good jobs and are successful, stuff like that. They used to tell us that when they were young, they used to struggle and there was racism. They used to teach stuff that was interesting.

When her family moved, Lavette's schooling experiences changed drastically. There were fewer African American students and teachers at her new high school. She rated the quality of instruction that she received during her junior and senior high school years as "fair," explaining that the classes were boring and "too teacher centered." Moreover, she did not believe that her teachers cared about her or liked her. She did think that they expected her to graduate but did not think that they expected her to become a successful adult. In contrasting her current high school versus previous high school, she said, "At my old school, it was like one big family. Everybody was like cool with everybody else. The teachers took their time and taught us. At this school, it's like I go from class to class. It's boring. I go to sleep in some of my classes and it's not interesting."

TYRONE

Like Lavette, Tyrone had also attended elementary school in another district besides the one where he attended high school, and he also attended two different high schools. He had already applied to a four-year university that had sent him three letters, and he dreamed of eventually becoming an FBI agent. Whereas Lavette experienced some school-related difficulties that stemmed from moving several times and having to make new friends again, Tyrone's biggest obstacle during elementary school was coping with the death of his mother. Thereafter, he was reared by an aunt. Regarding his mother's death, he said, "It didn't really hit me until I got older."

Although Tyrone felt that most of his elementary school teachers liked him, cared about him, and expected him to graduate and become a successful adult, he rated the quality of instruction that most of them provided as "fair." In his opinion, neither the course work nor homework prepared him for middle school. "It was a waste of time," he exclaimed, "because the things that they taught me in elementary, I didn't need to know in junior high. The course work was the same."

During middle school, Tyrone's aunt, grandmother, and some teachers started encouraging him to go to college. He rated the quality of instruction that he received as "good" and believed that most of his teachers cared about him, liked him, and expected him to graduate and to become a successful adult. Although Tyrone stated that neither his elementary school course work nor homework were sufficient to prepare him for middle school, he passed all his middle school classes.

Tyrone's first two years of high school were in the same district as his elementary and middle schools. Again, he rated the quality of instruction provided by most of his ninth and tenth grade teachers as "fair."

When he began to attend school in another neighboring city during eleventh grade, the quality of instruction improved. He rated the quality provided by most of his eleventh and twelfth grade teachers as "excellent." He also felt that most teachers at both schools had a positive opinion of him and of his future. At each level of his schooling, the teachers who made the greatest impact on him were teachers who formed a personal relationship with him and who were willing to provide extra help. The course work and homework that were most "beneficial" to him prepared him for the next level of his schooling. All other work, in his opinion, was meaningless.

SUMMARY

A recurring theme in this chapter has been that, first, the academic track that students were placed in and, second, retention during elementary school had a strong bearing on their schooling experiences. Students who were in G.A.T.E. or basic classes tended to have qualitatively different experiences than those who were in Special Education and/or who were retained, and even had different experiences from each other. For example, the majority of the students who completed the questionnaire rated the quality of instruction that they received in elementary school as "good." A higher percentage of Special Education students, however, gave it a low rating and a higher percentage of G.A.T.E. students gave it a high rating.

Sixty-one percent of the interviewees said that their elementary course work was "beneficial," but many said that it was only "somewhat beneficial" or "not beneficial." Of all the elementary grades, students were least likely to identify fourth grade as the grade when they had their easiest course work.

The statistically significant correlation between the grade in which students had their "worst" elementary teacher and the grade in which the course work was "most difficult" is revealing. This implies that students' "worst" elementary teachers may have made the course work more difficult through their attitudes and instructional practices. It is unlikely that these "worst" teachers "explained things well, made the course work interesting, provided extra help, or were patient," qualities that African American students associate with outstanding teaching. For example, in one of the two narratives in this chapter, Lavette describe her "worst" elementary teacher as an individual who punished students for doing their homework incorrectly. It appears that this teacher may have been unwilling to exercise the patience that is crucial to providing extra help to struggling students. Another elementary teacher, however, used a method that was more effective. She gave students a packet of homework on Monday and collected it at the end of the week. In so doing, she increased the likelihood of homework completion by giving students ample time to work on homework at their own pace.

Nearly half the students said that they received homework on a daily basis during elementary school, but 10 percent said that they only received it once or twice a week. A higher percentage of Special Education students received homework only once or twice per week. Conversely, a higher percentage of G.A.T.E. students received it four times per week. Moreover, students who received the most homework tended to be more satisfied with the overall quality of instruction provided by their elementary teachers.

Seventy percent of the students spent one to three hours per week on homework, but 7 percent said that they spent more than five hours per week on homework. Special Education students and elementary retainees tended to spend the least amount of time on homework, and G.A.T.E. students tended to spend the most.

About 40 percent of the students said that their homework was "beneficial," but the majority said that it was only "somewhat beneficial" or "not beneficial at all." Those who considered the homework to have been "beneficial" were more likely to have had their "best" teachers during an upper elementary grade. Students who received the most homework were more likely to assign a high rating to the quality of instruction that they received. Again, elementary retainees and Special Education students were at the opposite end from G.A.T.E. students. A higher percentage of G.A.T.E. students than others said that the homework was "beneficial" and a higher percentage of elementary retainees and Special Education students felt that it was only "somewhat beneficial" or "not beneficial" at all.

The results that were presented in this chapter illustrate the important role that students' elementary school track plays in the quality of their schooling experiences. The data indicate that elementary retainees and Special Education students tend to receive a substandard quality of instruction and less homework. Consequently, they also spend less time on homework. This is extremely important because African American students are disproportionately represented among Special Education students nationwide.

On the other hand, G.A.T.E. students are more likely to be satisfied with the quality of instruction they receive, tend to receive more homework, and tend to spend more time on homework during elementary school. Consequently, G.A.T.E. students are more likely to be prepared for middle or junior high school. At an early age, they have been given the prerequisites that are needed for academic success. They gain reinforcement by receiving homework frequently. They strengthen their study skills and knowledge base by devoting more hours to homework than other students. The qualitatively different caliber of instruction and the amount of homework that students receive in elementary school as a result of their academic track and whether or not they were retained appears to be another way in which inequality of educational opportunity is perpetuated.

Part II

Middle School Experiences

5

Middle School Issues

The middle school years are an enigmatic period in the American educational system. In many states, the traditional junior high school, which includes grades seven, eight, and nine, has almost become obsolete. Its replacement, the middle school, was designed to alleviate some of the problems that were associated with junior high school (Wiles & Bondi, 1998). The U.S. Department of Education (2000) reported that during the 1990s, the number of middle schools increased by 41 percent. Problems, however, continue to persist. Barr and Parrett (1995) said that middle schools rely on numerous practices that are detrimental to struggling students and they are too similar to high schools. Queen (1999) said that educators are still grappling with issues pertaining to where both sixth and ninth graders should be placed. This is evident in the number of kindergarten-through-fifth-grade versus kindergarten-through-sixth-grade elementary schools and the number of sixth-through-eighth-grade middle schools that exist.

Moreover, among the three levels of precollege educators, middle school teachers appear to be more likely than elementary or high school teachers to be singled out for criticism. For example, numerous studies have found that a higher percentage of middle school teachers tend to be underprepared for their teaching responsibilities (Barr & Parrett, 1995; Queen, 1999). Ingersoll (1999) reported that out-of-field teaching occurs in more than half of the secondary schools in the United States and over 4 million secondary students are taught by such teachers each year. He found that nearly one third of secondary teachers who teach math, one fourth of secondary English teachers, and one fifth of secondary science teachers did not major or minor in the subject that they were teaching, nor did they major or minor in a related subject. Ingersoll also revealed that high-poverty schools, small schools, and private schools were more likely than larger or affluent schools to have teachers who were teaching out-of-field. Within the same schools, students in Honors, Advanced Placement, and College Preparatory classes were less likely than others to be taught by teachers who were teaching out of their field. Furthermore, junior high or middle school students were more likely than high school students to have underprepared teachers. Ingersoll listed a number of negative consequences of out-of-field teaching that affect both teachers and students.

Regardless of the type of school that students attend after elementary school, starting middle school or junior high school is a major milestone. Leaving the elementary system in which students usually have one teacher per grade and going to middle school where students usually have multiple teachers can be overwhelming (Barr & Parrett, 1995). When family or social problems are added to the mix, this period can become even more stressful for students. At some point children become adolescents. During this period, they undergo physiological, emotional, and cognitive changes (Barr & Parrett, 1995; Queen, 1999). Queen (1999) stated that middle school students also feel insecure and alienated.

Barr and Parrett (1995) said that middle school students have a unique set of needs. Among these are the need for physical activity, diversity, positive social interaction with peers and adults, competence and achievement, and structure and limits. Successful middle schools, according to Barr and Parrett, have small learning communities, flexible block scheduling, interdisciplinary teams, parental involvement, and use students as resources to assist each other. Queen (1999) found that middle school students need lots of opportunities to interact with their peers and opportunities for "hands-on activities."

In addition to developmental changes that are associated with puberty that middle school students experience, peer pressure and academic demands also increase. For African American students, particularly males, middle school poses a unique set of circumstances. Although middle school students of all racial/ethnic groups experience numerous changes during this period, for African Americans the specter of racism affects their identity and self-concept and can result in anger and confusion (Comer & Poussaint, 1992; White & Parham, 1990). Moreover, during this period, African American youths can begin to have ambivalent feelings about American society and American values. On the one hand, they may feel included in society; on the other hand, they may feel excluded (Corbin & Pruitt, 1999). Furthermore, they must grapple with the contradictions between what they have been taught about American society and the reality of what it means to be an African

American in this society. This "duality" is at the center of identity development for African American youths who must find balance in the midst of conflicting messages (White & Parham, 1990).

Kunjufu (1990) described numerous ways in which schools destroy the self-esteem of Black boys. Among them are tracking, retention, limited assessment measures, and comparing the performance of boys to that of girls, even though the two groups develop at different rates. Whereas African American boys enter kindergarten with high self-esteem, their self-esteem at school decreases over time (Kunjufu, 1990; White & Parham, 1990). Kunjufu stressed, however, that school is one of the few places where African American boys have low self-esteem. Outside of school, they tend to exhibit high self-esteem.

Wilson (1987) said that the disconnectedness between school and the home lives of African American students can become a great source of psychological stress for students. Because schools are based on middle class behaviors and values, African American students from urban areas may perceive the school setting to be a "foreign establishment." At school, African American students see few links between the school culture and their own culture and way of speaking. Often, they do not see the long-term benefits of school either. Orange and Horowitz (1999) found that low teacher expectations are partly responsible for the "academic standoff" between African American and Hispanic male students and their teachers. Resistance to schooling is a common result.

During the preadolescent years, the peer group becomes very important to African Americans. This group may pressure other youths to adopt negative viewpoints of school and achievement. Some African American males may begin to associate school with femininity. Others may begin to act out in school or become more interested in sports or music. Additionally, adopting violent tendencies becomes a choice for some (Corbin & Pruitt, 1999). Two of the primary reasons African American children may adopt a violent or aggressive persona are the messages that they receive from some members of their community about violence and the messages that they receive from the media.

Within certain segments of the Black community, toughness or aggressiveness often leads to social status. As a result, some African American youths will also adopt violent characteristics, especially if they have poor coping skills to deal with racism and other forms of oppression (Corbin & Pruitt, 1999). Comer and Poussaint stated that in communities in which a great deal of fighting occurs, children become conditioned to viewing fighting as normal behavior. Payne (1998) stressed, however, that for children who come from impoverished environments, physical fighting is a tool that is required for survival in their communities. Therefore, it is incumbent on teachers to share strategies with students that will enable them to survive in the school environment, without resorting to physical violence.

Second, because the media in the United States tend to glorify violence and aggression, African American children infer that violence and aggression can lead to positive results. The U.S. Department of Education reported that during 1996, more than 60 percent of African American fourth graders attending public school said that they watched four or more hours of television per day (*Digest of Education Statistics*, 2000). For this reason, one can surmise that television has a huge impact on the ideas and values that African American children adopt. Furthermore, the more time that students spend watching television, the less time they have to spend on homework and recreational reading. Therefore, the inordinate amount of time that many African American children spend watching television may be linked to poor academic achievement as well as an internalization of messages that glorify violence.

The self-esteem and self-concept of African American youths are very important because they are linked to academic achievement. Because the middle-school years are challenging and a period when students experience many changes, these issues are pertinent to a discussion of this period of schooling. Additionally, educators, educational policies, and school practices can either increase or decrease self-esteem. There are several recurring themes in the literature regarding factors that contribute to academic achievement for African American students. One theme is that the self-esteem of African American youths and academic achievement improve when students have successful experiences at school and their success is reinforced (Comer & Poussaint, 1992; Corbin & Pruitt, 1999). Asa Hilliard said that the self-esteem of African American students increases when "they learn to do something that is valued by them and by others" and when they achieve "mastery over a new and difficult concept" (Mabie, 2000, 244).

Another theme is that a culturally relevant curriculum is extremely important to self-esteem, identity development, and academic achievement. African American students need to see people from their culture and backgrounds reflected in the texts that they read on an ongoing basis. Moreover, they need a curriculum that is connected to the real world in which they live. A third theme is that African American students tend to thrive in a collaborative versus competitive classroom environment. For this reason, cooperative learning groups are highly recommended (Comer & Poussaint, 1992; Kunjufu, 1990; Ladson-Billings, 1994; White & Parham, 1990). Another theme is that teacher expectations can have a positive or negative effect on achievement. Teachers with high expectations tend to have higher-achieving students (Comer & Poussaint, 1992; Kunjufu, 1990; White & Parham, 1990).

Because many African American students have routinely been subjected to low expectations and a watered down curriculum, high expectations are crucial for them. Kunjufu (1990) stressed that teachers'
expectations are much more important to the achievement of African
American students than are teachers' race and gender.

Davis and Jordan (1995) described several factors that contribute to
academic achievement among African American males in middle
school. Good study habits, attendance, and high teacher expectations
were all found to have positive correlations to achievement. Conversely, factors that served as deterrents to academic achievement
included an overreliance on discipline, retention, the need for remedi-
ation, suspension, and attending urban schools.

The 271 African American students who participated in the current
study were asked numerous questions about their middle school experiences. Ninety-four percent of the students said that they attended
middle or junior high school in California and nearly 90 percent attended a public school. Approximately 80 percent of the students were
in basic classes. A slightly lower percentage of middle school students
versus elementary students were in G.A.T.E. and a slightly lower percentage were in Special Education. When asked if they experienced any
major problems or obstacles during their middle school years that
might have prevented them from graduating or becoming a successful
adult, half of the interviewees said that they had, and girls accounted
for 79 percent of those who had. Family problems, conflicts with peers,
and difficulty in adjusting to middle school were the most frequently
cited problems.The narrative that follows illustrates why one of the
interviewees, an African American male, had difficulty adjusting to
both middle school and high school.

VINCENT

At the time of his interview, Vincent had applied to a university in
another state, saying that he wanted to go to college to improve his
financial situation. He had attended elementary, middle school, and
high school in the same school district and had both positive and
negative experiences to share. Although he was in basic classes during
elementary and middle school, in high school he took some college
preparatory classes.

Vincent rated the quality of instruction that most of his elementary
teachers provided as "good." He believed that most of his elementary
teachers cared about him and liked him but said that starting in fourth
grade, he disliked being at school. Although he received a lot of awards,

he was unsure of whether or not teachers believed that he would graduate or become a successful adult.

Whereas Vincent had conflicting thoughts about his elementary school experiences, his impressions of his middle school experiences were mostly negative. He rated the overall quality of instruction that he received as "poor." There were numerous discipline problems, and this decreased the amount of time that teachers spent on instruction. In some classes, the teachers "put the bad kids on one side and the good kids on the other side" of the classroom, Vincent said. In his own case, Vincent was moved back and forth across the room. "Somebody would say something stupid and I'd get into a fight and get into trouble," he explained.

Surprisingly, Vincent did believe that most of his middle school teachers liked him. "Usually, if I needed help or something, they would actually help you when you asked them," he said. "They always got on me if I didn't do my work." Conversely, Vincent didn't believe that most of his middle school teachers cared about him. "They would mostly try to give you Referrals," he said. He also believed that most of his middle school teachers did not expect him to graduate or become a successful adult. He attributed this to his personality and the way that he believed that other students perceived him. His belief that other students felt superior to him and his refusal to accept their attitude toward him culminated in an "attitude problem," according to Vincent. This was the major obstacle that he had to overcome during his middle school years. He explained:

> I did some stuff. I got in a lot of fights and stuff. I don't take a lot of stuff. I'll play with you or whatever, and I'll talk with you or whatever, but once I say something, I mean it. I don't like nobody talking down to me, you know what I mean? It wasn't too many teachers; it was more like students. They were talking down to me like I wasn't as smart as them. They either thought they were smarter, or they had to be big or bad all the time.

Because of his constant fighting, most of Vincent's middle school teachers assumed that he was a bad person, and for this reason they did not expect him to amount to much in life. In spite of this, he passed all his classes and earned enough credits to go to high school.

In comparison to his middle school experiences, high school was a more positive experience for Vincent. He attended two high schools in the same district and rated the quality of instruction as "good." He took college preparatory classes and said that most of his teachers seemed to think that he would graduate and eventually become a successful adult. However, he was unsure of whether or not they liked him or cared about him because of an incident that occurred during freshman year. This incident overshadowed the rest of his high school years and gave Vincent the impression that teachers feared him. The tension between Vincent and this World Geography teacher started on the first day of school and escalated. He explained:

> There was one teacher I had a problem with. He was messing with me the whole quarter. I think he didn't like me from the first day. He was like, "You play football?" and I said "Yea." He said, "So you gonna have trouble in class?" I had my jersey. It was my first day of tryouts. I kept telling my mom and she told me to stay in there, keep doing my work, and not to say anything. Whenever I was doing my work, he would stand over me. I would look up at him. Then, he'd say, "Don't look at me. Do your work." So, I would keep doing my work. And if he was standing around, he would always stare at me for no reason, with a mean look on his face.
>
> One day, he said I fronted him off. I had ringworm for a while and I had this beanie on because I was going to get my hair cut. It was raining. I took my hat off and sat it on my leg. The teacher tried to snatch it. I was trying to tell him what it was for and he got mad and snatched it from me. Then, he started writing a Referral for me.
>
> I had a jacket on, so I put my hood on. I was standing by the podium waiting for him and I guess he got scared when he saw me standing there. He ran to the phone and called security and security came to get me. The teacher said that I fronted him off and approached him in a mean manner or something like that. In other words, he said I tried to fight him. I hadn't done anything. I was just standing there. I might have looked mad. I probably was mad, but I don't believe in smart talking.

After that incident, according to Vincent, the teacher planned to press criminal charges against him. "He didn't want me in the school period," Vincent stressed. "He wanted me in jail." When Vincent's father, a retired police officer, went to the school and met with the teacher, the teacher decided not to press charges. "When he saw my dad, he got intimidated," Vincent explained. "My dad stood up to shake his hand and he got scared. My dad figured that [the incident] was because I'm Black and I'm big." It turned out that this teacher had a history of having problems with "big Black males," Vincent stated. In one case the previous year, the teacher and another large African American student got into a physical altercation. Vincent said that he noticed, however, that this teacher did not seem to have a problem with shorter Black male students.

As a result of this incident, Vincent concluded that most of his teachers had a negative impression of him that was driven by fear, mainly because of his size and dark skin. "I don't smile a lot," he said. "I'm kinda laid back. I just sit back and don't say too much. Like most people, teachers look at me and get kinda scared, but once I start talking, they're like, 'Oh.'"

In addition to failing the aforementioned World Geography class, Vincent failed two other classes during his freshmen year. Later, he made up these credits during summer school. At the time of his interview, a university in Washington had already contacted him about the possibility of awarding him a football scholarship. Vincent's goal was to major in math or science and eventually become a sports therapist.

SUMMARY

The middle school years are a time of transition and change. First, students must transition from the elementary school system in which they have had one teacher per year to a system requiring multiple teachers per year. Second, students must deal with numerous physiological and developmental changes. Peers become more influential, and self-esteem and identity issues are paramount. For African American students, these normal developmental phases are compounded by issues pertaining to racism, mixed messages about the United States, and what it means to be an American of African descent.

As illustrated through the narratives that have been presented throughout this book thus far, students' relationships with teachers are not only extremely important during elementary school, but they are also important during the secondary school years. In the case of Vincent, whose narrative was presented in this chapter, he received mixed messages from his middle school teachers. These teachers provided extra help but seemed preoccupied with discipline. In high school, a negative experience with a teacher who had "issues" with athletes and African American males who looked a certain way had a strong impact on him.

Like Vincent, other interviewees whose narratives have been presented thus far have mentioned that some teachers appeared to be too eager to hand out Referrals and seemed preoccupied with discipline. As Vincent stated about his middle school teachers, a preoccupation with discipline decreases the amount of instructional time. Obviously, in order to teach, teachers must have class control. However, an inordinate number of discipline problems is often a sign of a boring curriculum and ineffective instructional methods. For example, researchers have stressed that middle school students need frequent opportunities to interact with their peers and opportunities for physical activity (Barr & Parrett, 1995; Queen, 1999). Middle school teachers who rely on the traditional lecture model as their primary instructional method increase the likelihood that their students will become disruptive. Because students may undergo drastic personality changes during the middle school years and peer influence increases, a strong emphasis should be placed on conflict resolution and teaching students how to get along with their peers. Some classroom practices are actually conducive to this.

For example, Ladson-Billings (1994) said that successful teachers of African American children strive to develop a community of learners in their classrooms. These teachers encourage collaboration versus competition with one another. Instead of segregating students into smart versus dumb groups, these teachers empower students to "teach each other." Team effort and leadership skills are natural consequences of this pedagogy. More important, however, African American students can excel in this environment because the pressure to outperform others is minimized. Students feel "psychologically safe," and "they feel comfortable and supported" (p. 73). During middle school, Vincent did not appear to feel "psychologically safe." His belief that students were "talking down" to him because they felt intellectually superior to him resulted in conflicts with his peers.

Haberman (1995) stressed that "star" teachers of children in poverty do not spend an inordinate amount of time regurgitating facts and figures. They require students to become active participants in their learning by creating projects on an ongoing basis. White and Parham (1990) urged educators to create lessons that are based on problem-solving activities that address contemporary issues that are relevant to African American students' lives.

Finally, although the elementary school years represent an important period for African American students, the middle school years are equally important. Because of additional pressures that are compounded by a stronger awareness of the existence of racism, community attitudes against education, and the glorification of violence as an option, more attention should be given to these and other factors contributing to resistance to schooling by African American students. Teacher training programs must actively recruit more teachers, especially African Americans (Delpit, 1995), and equip them with the tools that will enable them to understand and successfully educate African American middle school students. There is a pressing need for a "critical mass" of African American educators at this level. African American educators are needed at all levels, but particularly in middle schools, because they will be more likely to understand the impact of racism on African American youths. They will also be more likely to be in a position to share effective coping strategies with students. Several of the interviewees whose narratives have been shared thus far, have stressed the strong positive impact that African American teachers have had on them. Unfortunately, as Delpit (1995) found, often teacher training institutions discourage instead of encourage African Americans who pursue education as a career. The result is a great loss for African American children in schools.

Although teachers of other races/ethnicities can also work effectively with African American students, as many of the narratives have illustrated, these teachers are at a disadvantage when they are ignorant of the sociocultural dynamics of African American life (Delpit, 1995; Ladson-Billings, 1994). Herein lies another weakness in standard teacher training programs and also in the educational system. Most educators are required to take one or two classes that deal with issues of diversity and cultural awareness. Often these courses merely scratch the surface. Moreover, some teachers are resistant to having to take such courses. Therefore, they enter the classes with a closed and negative mind-set, and they leave with the same negative mind-set. As a result, neither their attitude nor their behavior toward individuals from other backgrounds will change. Ladson-Billings (1994) said that many Americans are still reluctant to even acknowledge that African Americans have a separate and distinct culture. Hilliard (in Mabie, 2000) said that progress in race relations cannot be made until this reality is accepted.

Furthermore, even after teachers take required diversity and cultural awareness courses, the prevalence of institutional racism at the school in which they work often makes it easy for them to maintain negative attitudes and behaviors toward students from different racial/ethnic groups. When low expectations, disparaging remarks, and a low level of instruction are condoned at school, it becomes easier for teachers to ignore or forget what they learned in diversity and cultural awareness classes. In short, in order to close the achievement gap both teacher-training institutions and local educational policymakers must decide how to solve this dilemma. One very important step is finding a way to hold educators accountable for not only taking diversity and cultural awareness classes but also operationalizing what they learn in these courses. Until this occurs, many African American students will continue to bemoan the lack of a "critical mass" of African American teachers.

6

Middle School Teachers

BEST MIDDLE SCHOOL TEACHERS

Thirty-eight percent of the students who completed the questionnaire said that they had two or more "best" middle school teachers. This is higher than the percentage, 33 percent, who said that they had more than one "best" elementary teacher. A few said that they had so many outstanding middle school teachers that they could not say that one stood out as being superior to the rest. Others, however, said that they did not have any at all. For example, one student stated, "I can't remember the names of any of my middle school teachers."

More than half of the students said that an English/language arts teacher was the "best." The second most frequently cited answer was a social studies teacher. Table 6-1 provides more information about the students' answers to this question. The most common descriptions of "best" middle school teachers were that they appeared to care about their students, challenged students, made learning fun, gave extra help, made the subject matter comprehensible, or were African American.

For example, one boy said that his seventh grade history teacher was the "best" because "she was an African American teacher and it was motivational to me." Another student made a similar comment. She said that her seventh grade English teacher was the "best" because "she gave us so many hands-on activities. She was my first Black teacher and she was remarkable."

A second set of comments pertained to teachers who made learning fun. A student who was in basic classes during middle school said

TABLE 6-1
Best Middle School Teachers

Course Taught	Percentage of Students
1. Math	37
2. Science	35
3. Social Studies	42
4. English	53
5. Reading	16
6. Elective	29
7. P.E.	29

N = 271

Note: The percentage total exceeds 100 because some students identified more than one "best" teacher.

that his "best" teacher taught eighth grade history. His face lit up as he described her. "She was another one of those teachers who helped out a lot. She made everything fun and was in charge of other things that we did." A girl explained that her sixth grade science teacher was the "best" because he "taught so that everyone would understand him and he made the class enjoyable." A boy who took basic classes during middle school said that both his eighth grade English and eighth grade science teachers were the best "because I learned more from them. They had a way of making it fun and we did a lot of group projects." Another student said that her seventh grade history teacher "was fun. He got the class involved and asked us questions. He made learning a game." An eighth grade English teacher was the "best" because "he made it really fun and he gave out candy. He made you want to work hard."

"Challenge" was another theme that was associated with "best" teachers. A girl said that her P.E. teacher "was nice and would always push me to go as far as I could. He got close to my family, became a family friend, and we're still in touch." A boy said that his eighth grade social studies teacher "taught what he thought needed to be taught; he didn't stick to the regular curriculum." Another student said that her seventh grade teacher "taught all of the subjects. She cared a whole lot, and she wouldn't settle for second best."

As in previous chapters, having a caring attitude toward students and a positive attitude about teaching were also associated with "best" teachers. For example, one girl said that her seventh grade social studies teacher's attitude about life made her the "best." "She was just so up on exploring the world and just living life to the fullest." Regarding her eighth grade history teacher, a girl said, "He was just always there for me. I could always talk to him about anything." A seventh grade English teacher was the "best" because "she was dedicated and loved her students."

WORST MIDDLE SCHOOL TEACHERS

Sixteen percent of the African American students who completed the questionnaire said that they had two or more middle school teachers that they considered to be the "worst" of their teachers. This is slightly higher than the percentage, 14 percent, who said that they had more than one "worst" elementary teacher. On the other hand, a few students had no "worst" middle school teacher. Math and science teachers, respectively, were the most commonly cited choices for this category (see Table 6-2). "Worst" teachers tended to appear to be mean, grumpy, uncaring, boring, would not provide extra assistance, were preoccupied with discipline instead of teaching, unfair, or racist.

As in previous chapters, "meanness" and a bad attitude surfaced as characteristics of "worst" teachers. For example, a girl who was enrolled in basic middle school classes said that her eighth grade P.E. teacher was the "worst" because he "was mean for no reason." A boy said that his eighth grade science teacher "made the subject hard, didn't give much one-on-one help, and I didn't like him. I guess he was mean." A choir teacher was described as being "verbally abusive. He kicked me out of choir because I was sick. He was just bad." A girl said that her seventh grade math teacher qualified as her "worst" middle school

TABLE 6-2
Worst Middle School Teachers

Course Taught	Percentage of Students
1. Math	38
2. Science	35
3. Social Studies	25
4. English	17
5. Reading	9
6. Elective	13
7. P.E.	14

N = 271

Note: The percentage total exceeds 100 because some students identified more than one "worst" teacher.

teacher because "I felt like he was racist. A lot of people felt like he was racist. He was so grumpy."

Once again, a preoccupation with discipline instead of teaching surfaced as a quality of "worst" teachers. For example, a girl said that her eighth grade science teacher not only "gave Referrals to the office," but he made the curriculum boring. "He would talk and talk and talk, and just read straight out of the book." A boy complained that his eighth grade math teacher "had a really bad temper. He spent all of his time hollering at kids and throwing kids out." A girl said that her seventh grade social studies teacher "liked to give me Detention. I wasn't really disruptive, but I talked a lot." An eighth grade science teacher was considered the "worst" by one girl because "I'm not really into science. He had so many animals in there and it smelled. He was really dirty, the classroom was dirty, and everybody dreaded going in there." Another girl said that her eighth grade science teacher was the "worst" because "I hate science! The teacher felt that everybody should love science. She made me feel that if you don't love science, there's something wrong with you."

Another girl said that her eighth grade algebra teacher was the "worst" because "she'd get upset. A lot of people in that class really didn't understand and she tried to rush things." Another eighth grade social studies teacher was described as being unprepared and "the teaching didn't go together with what we were tested on sometimes. There was also a lack of class control."

Did Students Think That Most of Their Middle School Teachers Cared about Them?

Students who participated in the interview phase of the study were asked whether or not they thought that most of their middle school teachers cared about them personally. Fifty-four percent of the interviewees said that they felt that their middle school teachers cared about them. Conversely, 46 percent did not. These figures are very different from those pertaining to elementary teachers. Seventy-five percent of the students said that they thought that their elementary school teachers cared about them.

Students who believed that their middle school teachers cared about them tended to do so because the teachers made a personal connection with them and appeared to "go the extra mile" to help students succeed in school. Students who felt that their middle school teachers did not care about them tended to do so because they were given the impression that the teachers either did not like their jobs or did not want to be bothered with students. One girl said that the way in which the teachers "talked and acted" indicated to her that they did not care about her personally. Another student said that most of his middle school teachers "were just there for a paycheck." A student in basic classes said that her middle school teachers "didn't get to know students." One girl said, "I felt like an intruder in my middle school classes." A boy who took basic middle school classes said that his teachers were too busy giving discipline Referrals to care about students personally.

Did Students Believe That Most of Their Middle School Teachers Liked Them?

Eighty-five percent of the interviewees said that they believed that most of their middle school teachers liked them, compared to 82 percent who believed that their elementary teachers did. On the other hand, 15 percent believed that most of their middle school teachers disliked them. Both groups based their answer to this question on their interpersonal relationships with middle school teachers. For example, one student said that she believed that most of her middle school teachers liked her because they taught her "how to get along with other people and how to make myself more outgoing " Another student said that her middle school teachers would joke with her and telephone her home when she began to fall behind academically. Those who felt that most of their middle school teachers disliked them believed that the teachers were only there for a paycheck or did not appear to be interested in students. Only one G.A.T.E. student said that the majority of her teachers disliked her during middle school. The rest who gave that answer were non-G.A.T.E. students.

Did Students Think That Most of Their Middle School Teachers Believed That They Would Graduate from High School?

Seventy-five percent of the interviewees thought that their middle school teachers believed that they would graduate from high school, compared to 86 percent who said that their elementary teachers believed that they would graduate. Only one G.A.T.E. student felt that her middle school teachers did not expect her to graduate. A student who took basic middle school classes said that she did not know if her teachers expected her to graduate because "they didn't really talk to us about high school." A boy said that his middle school teachers did not think that he'd graduate because he "got into lots of fights." Another boy said that his teachers expected him to graduate because "I was a leader." Another boy said that he thought his middle school teachers believed that he would graduate because "they pushed."

Did Students Think That Most of Their Middle School Teachers Believed That They Would Become Successful Adults?

Seventy-one percent of the interviewees said that their middle school teachers believed that they would become successful adults. A slightly higher percentage, 75 percent, believed this about their elementary school teachers. Some students said that they did not know or they did not think that their middle school teachers thought that they would become successful adults. For example, one student said, "I didn't get to know them. I was just a quiet student who sat in back." The following narrative provides another glimpse into the elementary and secondary schooling experiences of one of the African American students who participated in the interview phase of the study.

SHANAE

At the time of her interview, Shanae, who took mostly basic classes from elementary through high school, was one of the few interviewees who had no plans to go to college. Her dream was to join the Air Force, but she was lacking credits toward graduation. Although she "almost failed fourth grade," most of her elementary school experiences were positive. She said, "Everything was easy to me until fourth grade. I almost flunked and that kind of taught me to think of school more. I think it was my math, because I wasn't getting my math right. Everything else was okay. It was just my math. I don't know if it was the teachers or me, but it was just fourth grade where I had problems." Shanae attended two different elementary schools in contiguous school districts and rated the quality of instruction that most of her teachers provided as "fair." She had mixed feelings about her elementary teachers. Whereas she believed that most of them cared about her, liked her, and believed that she would graduate from high school, she also felt that most of them did not expect her to become a successful adult.

Shanae described her middle school years as "pretty fun," in spite of the fact that she attended three different schools. Furthermore, she was harassed continuously by another student. She explained:

> A boy that I went to elementary school with and I never got along. One day, I was walking across the street from school and he came and jumped on my back. I was telling him to get off of me and everybody was laughing at me. I fell to the ground and he threw marijuana all in my face. After that, he and two others started following me. My friend was right there but she didn't do anything. I was like, "Oh my God!" They were in back of me the

whole time and I was just crying. I got to my house and told my grandma. We took it to school the next day and it was like from that day on, it seemed like he wasn't really harassing me, but I would hear little smart stuff, like I'm a "tattle tale" and all kinds of stuff. He wasn't suspended or anything. I never was scared of him but I just didn't like the fact that I would have to hear it. I felt uncomfortable at the school when I walked past him.

Shanae stated that ongoing conflicts with this boy were the biggest problems that she experienced during her middle school years. Eventually, she had to leave the school and transfer to a private school. "I went to private school for all of eighth grade," she said. "I felt like I was an intruder. I felt like I shouldn't even be there, because all those kids were there from kindergarten until their eighth grade year, and all of a sudden I just come in there during eighth grade. I didn't have friends but I didn't care. I felt like everybody was against me because I was new and they had known each other since they were little."

Like the quality of instruction provided by most of her elementary school teachers, Shanae rated that of middle school as "fair." This was even true of the private school, where, she said, "the work was actually easier. We stayed in one class. I did fine with my grades." Moreover, she was uncertain of whether or not the course work or homework that she received was "beneficial."

Although she sensed that most of her middle school teachers liked her, Shanae did not believe that they cared about her. "I think they did what they had to do," she stated. "I don't think that they tried to get to know the students." Moreover, even though she did not fail any of her middle school courses, she was unsure of whether or not her teachers expected her to graduate from high school or become a successful adult.

This ambivalence also surfaced when she was asked to describe her "best" and "worst" middle school teachers. Shanae could not remember having one outstanding teacher during this time. She did, however, remember the "worst" of her middle school teachers. "Mrs. R. taught seventh grade Sex Education," Shanae stated. "She was another one with an attitude. If you asked her a question, she just gave you a totally bad attitude and the work was kind of hard."

In high school, the quality of instruction that most of her teachers provided was an improvement over that of previous years. Therefore, Shanae rated it as "good." During ninth grade, she took college preparatory classes and failed every single class, except for P.E. "I wasn't taking my classes seriously, not at all," she admitted. I just wasn't applying myself. I didn't do homework. I was being lazy. I got one A and that was in P.E. I'm athletic. I played basketball in tenth grade and ran track last year." Thereafter, she took Basic classes. During tenth grade, she failed an English class. "The teacher didn't want to explain things twice," Shanae said. "She was another one of those teachers who had an attitude problem." This, however, was the last class that Shanae failed.

Most of her high school teachers appeared to like her and care about her. Although Shanae felt that they believed that she would graduate, again, she was unsure of whether or not they expected her to become a successful adult. The one teacher who made the greatest impact on her was a twelfth grade government teacher who made the class fun and invited lots of guest speakers. "He wanted us to succeed," Shanae said. Among the guest speakers were college students and representatives from the military. Although her government teacher, who was the first and only educator to do so, encouraged Shanae to apply for college, she decided that the military would be more interesting and beneficial. For this reason, her goal was to join the Air Force after graduation.

SUMMARY

In the previous chapter, peer relations and relationships between students and teachers surfaced as important dimensions of the schooling experiences of African American middle school students. In the current chapter, the important role of teachers in exacerbating or ameliorating schooling experiences was underscored once again. This has been a recurring theme regarding both the elementary and middle school experiences of African American students.

When asked to identify their "best" middle school teachers, more than half of the 271 students who completed the questionnaire identified an English/language arts teacher. Social studies teachers were the second most frequently cited group of "best" middle school teachers. Moreover among the teachers who taught core or required subjects, English/language arts teachers were least likely to be cited as "worst" teachers. Conversely, math and science teachers were most likely to be cited as "worst" middle school teachers. The "best" middle school teachers appeared to care about students, challenged them, gave extra help, explained things well, and made learning fun. The "worst" teachers were boring, uncaring, did not get to know students personally, had bad attitudes, or would not provide extra help.

Using the list of characteristics of outstanding teachers that the majority of students deemed most important (see chapter 3), several conclusions or assumptions can be made. Because the majority of the African American students said that outstanding teachers "explain things well" and "make the course work interesting," one can assume that the "best" middle school teachers for African American students possess these characteristics.

Another assumption that can be made is that English/language arts and social studies teachers are more likely than math or science teachers to "explain things well" and "make the course work interesting" to African American middle school students. A third assumption is that the "best" middle school teachers for African American students "give extra help," are "patient," "fair," "friendly," and use "humor" in their method of delivery. It appears that English/language arts and social studies teachers are also more likely than math or science teachers to possess these qualities. Another possibility is that in English/language arts and social studies classes, African American students are more likely to see other African Americans reflected in the textbooks through literature and historical events than in math or science classes. Regardless of why English/language arts and social studies teachers were more likely than math or science teachers to be selected as "best" middle school teachers, it is clear that these teachers are using personal qualities and instructional practices that African American students value.

Several interviewees mentioned that their "best" middle school teacher was an African American. This was the first time that some students had an African American teacher. Students' related comments imply, as noted in the previous chapter, that good African American teachers are needed and can have a positive impact on African American students.

Several students also stressed that their "worst" middle school teachers were preoccupied with discipline. Some students even felt that certain teachers were looking for reasons to send kids to the office. Haberman (1995) said that the best teachers in impoverished schools do the opposite. They are proactive, instead of reactive, and discipline is not one of their top priorities. Instead, outstanding teachers create a classroom environment that makes learning, versus discipline, the primary focus. Moreover, these teachers get to know each student on a personal level before any discipline problems occur.

Another pattern that has begun to emerge from the narratives and other comments from students is that asking questions is discouraged by some teachers. Numerous students have stated that certain teachers did not want them to ask questions. This proves to be particularly problematic, because it is the opposite of one of the characteristics that African American students value in good teachers. Obviously, if students have questions, the assignment or topic was not "explained well." If a teacher refuses to answer questions or dissuades students from asking them, students will remain confused. This confusion can affect students' academic performance and classroom behavior. Low achievement and discipline problems can become direct results.

The interviewees were also asked additional questions about their middle school teachers. More than half of the interviewees said that they believed that most of their middle school teachers cared about them; 75 percent said that they believed that their elementary teachers cared about them. Eighty-five percent of the interviewees believed that most of their middle school teachers liked them compared to 82 percent who believed that their elementary teachers did.

A pattern that has emerged in this and previous chapters is that being "liked" by teachers does not necessarily ensure that teachers "care." Many students commented that although their elementary and middle school teachers appeared to "like" them, they still did not feel that these teachers really cared about their welfare or cared about them as human beings. This is an important point to note, because a teacher who cares about African American students will be more likely to offer students the type of curriculum, the quality and type of instruction, and the extra assistance that these students need to truly improve the quality of their lives. Moreover, Shanae's narrative indicates that some African American students really do not know how their teachers feel about them—one way or the other.

A lower percentage of students thought that most of their middle school teachers expected them to graduate from high school than those who believed that their elementary teachers did. Seventy-one percent said that most of their middle school teachers thought they would become successful adults compared to 75 percent who thought that their elementary teachers did. It is clear that a higher percentage of interviewees had positive beliefs regarding their elementary school teachers' viewpoints of them. Moreover, G.A.T.E. students were more likely than others to believe that most of their middle school teachers liked them and expected them to graduate from high school. Many of the G.A.T.E. students who participated in the interview phase of the study had attended the aforementioned prestigious public preparatory school. The quality of their middle school experiences appeared to be markedly superior to those of other interviewees.

A recurring theme in this chapter has been that whereas many middle school teachers "possess the right ingredients" to ensure that they will be successful with African American students, others need assistance. The comments that some students who participated in the current study made regarding their "worst" middle school teachers indicate that teacher preparation programs and professional growth workshops for educators must devote more time to teaching middle school teachers how to improve the ways in which they relate to African American students.

7

Middle School Course Work and Homework

The students who completed the questionnaire were asked several questions about their middle school course work and homework. Interviewees were asked additional questions. Fifteen percent of the students who completed the questionnaire said that they failed at least one course during middle school. Students who were in G.A.T.E. during elementary school were least likely to have failed a middle school course.

Those who failed courses were more likely to fail math or science classes, and least likely to fail reading, physical education, or elective courses. Seventy-three percent of the students who failed a class during middle school failed math. More than half of those who failed a class failed science, and nearly half of those who failed failed social studies.

MOST DIFFICULT MIDDLE SCHOOL COURSE

Although the majority of the students who participated in the study did not fail any middle school course, all students found at least one course to be difficult. Math and science were the two most challenging middle school courses for students. Moreover, the majority of the students in the study said that math was challenging for them. Students were least likely to struggle with physical education and their elective classes. Twenty percent of the students identified more than one course as being "most difficult." Table 7-1 provides more information about the students' responses to this question.

TABLE 7-1
The Most Difficult Middle School Courses for Students

Course	Percentage of Students
1. Math	65
2. Science	41
3. Social Studies	26
4. English	20
5. Reading	6
6. Elective	4
7. P.E.	3

N = 271

Note: Because many students circled more than one answer, the percentage total exceeds 100.

EASIEST MIDDLE SCHOOL COURSE

The students who completed the questionnaire were most likely to say that physical education, an elective class, or English/language arts was their "easiest" middle school course. They were less likely to identify math, science, reading, or social studies as their "easiest" course. Table 7-2 provides more information about students' responses to this question.

BENEFITS OF MIDDLE SCHOOL COURSE WORK

Students who participated in the interview phase of the study were also asked whether or not most of their middle school course work

TABLE 7-2
The Easiest Middle School Courses for Students

Course	Percentage of Students
1. Math	35
2. Science	35
3. Social Studies	38
4. English	50
5. Reading	35
6. Elective	52
7. P.E.	66

N = 271

Note: Because many students circled more than one answer, the percentage total exceeds 100.

was "beneficial." Most students felt that their course work was beneficial, but 21 percent disagreed. Conversely, 36 percent had stated that their elementary school course work was only "somewhat beneficial" or "not beneficial" at all. In general, those who thought that their middle school course work had been helpful said that it had prepared them for high school. Those who did not said that the course work was "busy work," or it had not prepared them for high school. One student, however, said that some of his classes were lacking supplies that were needed.

THE OVERALL QUALITY OF INSTRUCTION PROVIDED BY MIDDLE SCHOOL TEACHERS

More than half, 56 percent, of the questionnaire respondents rated the overall quality of instruction that their middle school teachers provided as "good," and 13 percent rated it as "excellent." Twenty-seven percent rated it as "fair," and only 3 percent gave it a "poor" rating. There was a moderate statistically significant correlation between students' academic track during elementary and middle school and how they rated the quality of instruction that they received during middle school ($r = .46$; $p < .01$). A higher percentage of G.A.T.E. students rated it as "good" or "excellent." A higher percentage of students who were retained and/or in Special Education during elementary school than others rated it as "poor" or "fair" (see Table 7-3). One student said that the quality of instruction that most of his middle school teachers provided was "good" because "they helped in class and after school." Another student said that it was "good" because "they taught me how to do the work."

TABLE 7-3
How Students Rated the Quality of Instruction Provided by Their Middle School Teachers

	Poor	Fair	Good	Excellent
Elementary Track		(%)		
Total Sample of Students	3	27	56	13
Retainees	8	31	49	12
Special Ed.	9	36	46	9
Basic	3	31	55	11
G.A.T.E.	2	13	61	19

N = 271

THE NUMBER OF DAYS PER WEEK THAT
STUDENTS RECEIVED HOMEWORK

Sixty percent of the students said that their middle school teachers assigned homework on a daily basis. Twenty-one percent said that they received homework at least four times per week. A higher percentage of students who were in G.A.T.E. versus Special Education or basic classes during elementary school received homework four times per week. A higher percentage of students who were not in G.A.T.E. during elementary school received homework daily. Only 1 percent of the total sample of students received homework once a week, and 2 percent of the G.A.T.E. students did (see Table 7-4).

THE AMOUNT OF TIME THAT STUDENTS SPENT
ON THEIR MIDDLE SCHOOL HOMEWORK

The majority of the students spent two to five hours per week on homework during middle school, but 14 percent spent more than seven hours per week on homework. The amount of time that students spent on homework during middle school varied according to the track that they were in during elementary school. For example, those who were in Special Education or retained during elementary school were more likely than those who were in basic or G.A.T.E. to report that they spent three hours or less on homework. Those who were in G.A.T.E. or basic classes were more likely than those who were in Special Education or who were retained during elementary school to report that they spent six or more hours per week on homework. There was a low statistically significant correlation between the amount of time that students spent on homework during middle school and how they rated the quality of instruction that most of their middle school teachers provided ($r = .20$;

TABLE 7-4
The Number of Days per Week That Students Received Homework during Middle School

	One	Two	Three	Four	Daily
Elem. Track/and Retention			%		
Total Sample	1	3	14	21	60
Retainees	0	12	8	12	68
Special Ed.	0	9	9	27	55
Basic	1	3	14	19	62
G.A.T.E.	2	14	27	54	2

N = 271

TABLE 7-5
The Number of Hours per Week That Students Spent on Homework Assignments during Middle School (by % of Students, Retainees, and Their Elementary Track)

Elem. Track	1 or less	2–3	4–5	6–7	8–9	10 or more
Total Sample	13	37	25	10	7	7
Retainees	15	46	19	4	8	4
Special Ed.	27	46	18	0	0	9
Basic	13	39	23	10	7	6
G.A.T.E.	7	27	30	13	7	9

N = 271

$p < .001$). In other words, students who spent the most time on home-work were more likely than those who spent less time on homework to give a high rating to the quality of instruction. Table 7-5 provides more information about the students' responses.

BENEFITS OF MIDDLE SCHOOL HOMEWORK

The majority of students did not feel that their middle school home-work assignments were very beneficial. Forty-three percent felt that they were "beneficial," but half of the students thought that they were only "somewhat beneficial." Students who were in G.A.T.E. during elementary school were more likely than those who were retained or in elementary Special Education or basic classes to say that either the homework was "beneficial" or it was "not beneficial" at all (see Table 7-6). There was a low statistically significant correlation between the amount of homework that students received during middle school and whether or not students felt that the homework was "beneficial" ($r = .22$; $p < .001$). A student who was in basic classes during middle school

TABLE 7-6
How Students Rated the Benefits of Their Middle School Homework (by % of Students, Retainees, and Their Elementary Track)

Elem. Track	Not Beneficial	Somewhat Beneficial	Beneficial
Total Sample	5	50	43
Retainees	4	62	27
Special Ed.	0	63	27
Basic	4	54	40
G.A.T.E.	9	34	55

N = 271

explained, "A lot of it didn't really have to do with high school. A lot of it was too easy. It was like child's play." A G.A.T.E. student who attended the public, yet highly selective and competitive, preparatory school said, "The homework was terrible. There was too much. There should be a balance." Another student who was in basic classes said that the homework "wasn't explained enough." The narrative that follows describes the elementary and secondary schooling experiences of another student who participated in the interview phase of the study.

JAVON

At the time of his interview, JaVon, who wanted to become a hotel or restaurant manager, had applied to a local four-year university. Although he had taken basic classes in elementary, middle, and high school instead of college preparatory classes, he was determined to go to college. Starting in elementary school, his family and a fifth grade teacher began stressing the importance of college to him. "My family is expecting me to go to college," he said. "I have to do it for them. My grandmother really wants me to go. My parents, they really want me to go, and of course, I have to go to school to make my money, basically."

Like many of the interviewees, JaVon had positive memories of his elementary school years. He attended a public school in Los Angeles and believed that most of his teachers liked him and cared about him. He also believed that most of his elementary teachers expected him to graduate from high school and to become a successful adult. "They really did care about their job," he stated. "They were there to teach and they cared about teaching. Some of the teachers in elementary were better than any of the teachers I've ever had. They made sure that I learned." As a result, JaVon rated the overall quality of instruction provided by most of his elementary teachers as "good."

Middle school was different. He had mixed feelings about his teachers' perceptions and expectations of him. In JaVon's opinion, most of his middle school teachers did not care about him. "Most were just there for a paycheck," he said. "Most of them could have done a little bit more. It was just a basic job to them. No one really wanted to put up with the bad kids that weren't worth it." Although he believed that most of his middle school teachers liked him personally, he did not believe that they expected him to graduate from high school or become a successful adult. "Like I said," he stated, "there were a lot of teachers who were just there for a paycheck. They didn't care anything about me."

One teacher who taught eighth grade social studies stood out in JaVon's mind. He was JaVon's "best" middle school teacher because "he taught what needed to be taught and he put everything into teaching." Another teacher who stood out in JaVon's mind taught eighth grade math. JaVon considered him to be his "worst" middle school teacher because "he had a really bad temper. He spent all of his time hollering at kids and throwing kids out of class. He would talk about kids and actually fight them." In spite of the fact that JaVon earned passing grades in all his middle school classes and thought that most of the homework and course work were "beneficial," he rated the overall quality of instruction that he received during middle school as "fair."

Compared to his middle school experiences, high school was an improvement. The quality of instruction was better. He felt that most of his teachers cared about him, liked him, expected him to graduate, and believed that he would become a successful adult. As in middle school, JaVon earned passing grades in all his high school classes.

A twelfth grade teacher made a positive impact on JaVon during a difficult period. He explained, "Mr. B. cares about you like he's your father. I couldn't have made it through high school without him. I've known him since tenth grade. I was really shy. I was closed off to the world. He gave me so many different skills that would get me to survive in life. He's like my father basically."

SUMMARY

The feedback that the students provided regarding several aspects of their middle school years yielded several noteworthy results. Differences between elementary and middle school experiences became evident. For example, whereas 10 percent of the students failed a grade during elementary school, 15 percent failed at least one middle school course. Those who failed were most likely to fail a math or science course.

The higher percentage of students who failed at least one middle school course might be explained in one of several ways. First, students who failed during middle school might have struggled with the same subject(s) during elementary school but may have earned enough passing grades in other subjects to be promoted to the next grade. For example, at least two interviewees said that they struggled with math during elementary school. One was actually retained during third grade, and the other said that she was almost retained during fourth grade as a result of problems with math.

Another plausible explanation is that students who failed a middle school course may have received inadequate preparation, particularly in math and science, during elementary school. After all, nearly 40 percent of the interviewees stated that their elementary course work was only "somewhat beneficial" or "not beneficial" at all. Additionally, a number of researchers have found a high percentage of poorly qualified math and science teachers in secondary schools (Drew, 1996; Ingersoll, 1999; Wenglinsky, 2000), so this is highly possible. Moreover, math and science were the most difficult middle school subjects for most of the students. Still another possibility is that the adjustment problems that some students experienced during the middle school years may have affected their school performance.

Conversely, whereas many of the African American students struggled with math and/or science during middle school, English/language arts was the "best" subject for most. One reason might be that math and English/language arts require different skills. Perhaps the students received a stronger language arts foundation in elementary school, thereby increasing the likelihood that they would do well in this subject during middle school. Another alternative is that the students might have found English/language arts with its strong emphasis on literature to be more appealing than math and/or science. Another possibility, as noted in the previous chapter, is that the middle school English/language arts teachers may have exemplified the characteristics of outstanding educators that African American students deem to be most important. After all, more than half of the students said that their "best" middle school teacher taught English/language arts. Conversely, of all the middle school core subject teachers, math teachers were most likely to be deemed the "worst." Thus, "easiest" middle school core subjects were correlated to "best" middle school teachers. In other words, the way the subject was taught appears to have been a strong determinant of course difficulty.

In spite of the fact that many students struggled with math and science during middle school, most gave a high rating to the overall quality of instruction provided by their middle school teachers. Again, students who were in G.A.T.E. during elementary school versus those who were retained or in lower elementary tracks were more likely to assign a high rating to it.

Although most students felt that their middle school homework was only "somewhat beneficial," students who were in G.A.T.E. during elementary school were more likely than others to find it "beneficial." Most students received homework on a daily basis during middle school, but a higher percentage of students who were in G.A.T.E. versus other tracks during elementary school received it four times per week. Some G.A.T.E. students even received homework only once or twice per week. This indicates that requirements and expectations for G.A.T.E. students may vary and lack uniformity or that the students had moved to lower tracks by middle school.

There was a statistically significant correlation between the amount of time that students spent on their middle school homework and how they rated the quality of their middle school instruction. Just as students who were in G.A.T.E. during elementary school were more likely than others to spend more time on their middle school homework, these students were also more likely to express satisfaction with the overall quality of their middle school instruction. Although the majority of students in the study spent two to five hours per week on their middle school homework, those who were in Special Education or retained during elementary school were more likely than others to spend less time on homework.

In short, there were only slight differences between the value that students placed on their elementary versus middle school homework. In both cases, when the percentage of students who rated the homework as "somewhat beneficial" is combined with the percentage who said that it was "not beneficial," it becomes evident that there is a need to improve the type, quality, and amount of homework that is assigned to elementary and middle school African American students.

Part III

High School Experiences

8

High School as an
Ending and a Beginning

For many students, high school is the beginning of the end of their
formal schooling years. For others, it is the last stop before college.
Undoubtedly, the quality of elementary and middle school experiences that students have had will impact their high school experiences, as indicated by the narratives in previous chapters. Students
who have been "tracked" for college have in essence been selected
to move in the direction of joining the middle or professional class.
Those who have not are more likely to be relegated to lower paying
jobs or unemployment.

According to Barr and Parrett (1995), high school can be problematic
for a number of reasons. First, most high schools are still biased toward
serving the needs of college-bound students. Therefore, they are less
likely to prepare non-college-bound students to graduate with voca-
tions that will help them gain access to jobs. Second, high school can
exacerbate the problems of students who come from impoverished and
troublesome home environments. Because of tracking and poor instruction, these students often enter high school lacking the skills that are
crucial for academic success. The result is often anger and resistance to
schooling.

Inadequate schooling can manifest itself in several ways at the high
school level, particularly for many African American students who,
according to NAEP, leave high school with the skills that are equivalent
to those of White middle school students. One way is through poor
reading skills. Because most high school textbooks have a high readability level, strong reading skills are crucial for academic success.
Consequently, students who enter high school with poor reading skills

are more likely to fall behind. Moreover, poor reading skills among high school students is a widespread problem. For example, whereas approximately 20 percent of the high school seniors nationwide read below the basic level, higher percentages of African American and Hispanic seniors do so (National Center for Education Statistics, 1999).

Roe, Stoodt, and Burns (1998) said that ninth graders' reading levels can range anywhere from five grades below grade level to five grades above grade level. They differentiated among three main types of adolescent readers. "Developmental readers" can read textbooks that are written at grade level. Therefore, instruction that is geared toward helping them refine their reading skills is beneficial. "Corrective readers" may read at around 18 months below grade level and can read content area textbooks with assistance from the teacher. "Remedial readers" read two or more years below grade level and need the assistance of a reading specialist to work with them on basic reading skills.

Gillet and Temple (2000) found that adolescents who read below grade level suffer not only academically but socially as well. These problems can lead to disruptive behavior and to an increased likelihood of dropping out of school. Unfortunately, the reading problems of secondary students often go undetected or unremediated because most secondary teachers have not been trained to teach reading skills (Thompson, 2000). Celeste's story in chapter 2 provides a graphic illustration of the effect of poor reading skills on elementary and secondary schooling experiences.

Weak math skills can also become exacerbated at the high school level. Students who missed basic math concepts in elementary and/or middle school are likely to continue to struggle with math. This is particularly true of African American students. In 1999, although nearly 90 percent of African American 17-year-olds nationwide were proficient in numerical operations and beginning problem solving, less than 30 percent were proficient in moderately complex procedures and reasoning, as measured by NAEP. Furthermore only 1 percent were proficient at multistep problem solving and algebra (U.S. Department of Education, 2000).

Polite (1999) conducted a study involving African American males who attended a suburban high school. One of his major findings was that the students felt that the majority of their counselors and teachers had not challenged them academically, particularly in math. The students also believed that counselors and teachers had failed to provide a "caring school environment." Polite concluded that these students' high school experiences mirrored those of countless African Americans nationwide. Additionally, the racial composition of the students' high school was a key determinant of the quality of instruction and amount of guidance that they received.

As noted previously, Drew (1996) discussed the effects of un-derprepared math and science teachers on students' skills. He cited many studies, including his own work, that stressed how students are affected by the quality of math and science instruction that they receive. He also underscored the link between math preparation and college achievement and emphasized that good math skills may be the key determinant of academic achievement in college. Drew also argued that because math and science are gatekeeping subjects to prestigious colleges and universities, as well as to lucrative careers, inadequate math and science preparation not only contributes to poor achievement in college but it also widens the economic gap between the poor and individuals from a higher socioeconomic status. He concluded that in order to improve math and science education, more qualified teachers should be hired, teachers should believe that every student can master math and science, and teachers should utilize cooperative study groups. Cooperative study groups have been found to greatly increase the math achievement levels of students of color.

Like Drew (1996), Wenglinsky (2000) and the contributors to the annual report Quality Counts (2000), found that the quality of instruc-tion that students receive is directly linked to teacher preparedness in that teachers who majored or minored in the subjects that they teach are more likely to produce high-performing students. One of Wenglinsky's main findings was that math and science teachers do not receive enough professional development to assist them in meeting the needs of "special student populations." When math teachers do receive professional development to assist them with these students, their students make great strides.

In addition to problems stemming from inadequate elementary or middle school preparedness, high school students also face other prob-lems. Just as middle school students experience a unique set of prob-lems relating to puberty, peer pressure, and adjusting to having multiple teachers versus one teacher per year, high school students are more likely than others to become involved in practices that can have long-term effects. For example, among eighth, tenth, and twelfth grad-ers, illicit drug use increases with age. Whereas about 27 percent of eighth graders reported using illegal drugs in 2000, 54 percent of high school seniors did so (U.S. Department of Health, 2000). Paradoxically, although a higher percentage of White than African American eighth and twelfth graders reported that they used illegal drugs, alcohol, or smoked cigarettes (National Institute on Drug Abuse, 2000), African American students are more likely to be perceived as discipline prob-lems, and to be suspended and expelled from school.

As with substance abuse, pregnancy rates also increase with age. Older students are more likely than younger girls to become pregnant.

Moreover, African American and Hispanic teens, particularly those ranging in age from 15 to 17, have higher birth rates than their counterparts of other races or ethnicities (National Vital Statistics Reports, 1999).

The 271 students who completed the questionnaire for the current study answered numerous questions about their high school years. Approximately 90 percent of the students attended public high schools for all four years, but a few spent one or two years at private high schools. Furthermore, some students attended high schools in two or more districts. Nearly 40 percent of the students were in basic or college preparatory classes. Twelve percent were in G.A.T.E., Honors, or Advanced Placement classes, and 4 percent were in Special Education classes. The percentage of students who were in G.A.T.E. during elementary school (21 percent) had decreased substantially by high school (12 percent). The percentage of students who were in Special Education during elementary school remained the same.

The majority of the students had a cumulative grade point average ranging from 2.0 to 3.9. A higher percentage of students who were in G.A.T. E. during elementary school (55 percent) had a 3.0 or higher grade point average. Nearly 40 percent of students who took basic elementary classes had a 3.0 or higher grade point average. Students who were in Special Education (9 percent) and/or retained during elementary school (23 percent) were least likely to have a 3.0 or higher high school grade point average.

When asked if they had experienced any major obstacles or problems during high school, 64 percent of the interviewees said, "yes." A much higher percentage of girls than boys said that they had experienced a major problem or obstacle. Family problems, low grades, the death of a loved one, personal problems, or conflicts with peers or teachers were the most frequently cited problems that students experienced. Ninth grade appeared to be a period when many students had difficulty adjusting to high school. The following narrative is based on an interview with a student who experienced major problems during elementary, middle, and high school.

KADIJA

At the time of her interview, Kadija, who is half Black and half White, had already applied to a local four-year university. After spending four years in ROTC, she dreamed of joining the military or working in law enforcement, but a health condition made both dreams unlikely. She had spent most of her elementary and middle school years in Los Angeles County schools. Because she had moved a lot, she had only been in her current school district for one and a half years. She was currently living with her father, an African American, and her step-mother, who is White. Regarding why she designated herself as "Black" or "African American," Kadija stated, "Most of the time when people first see me they think that I'm Cuban. If you want to get down to the nitty gritty, it's the one drop of blood, so I'm Black. Otherwise, my father's Black and my mother's Caucasian. Usually, when they put 'Other' on forms, I put 'Black,' because it's too complicated, you know." During each level of her schooling, Kadija had taken basic classes. Of all her years in school, her elementary years were probably the most challenging. In addition to constant moving, her biological parents were embroiled in custody battles. Kadija explained:

I attended a lot of elementary schools. The reason we moved so much was because of money and a lack of funds. We struggled a lot. My father and my stepmother were both drinking at the time. We moved around a lot. I was having a lot of problems with my biological mother because she would always have a custody battle. When I was eight years old she had custody of me and my brother for a year and throughout that entire year we were physically, mentally, and sexually abused. Before that, most of the time, I was with my father.

My father admits that he used to beat my mother and we think that her abuse of us had something to do with that. And some of it has to do with racism. Some people say that it may not be, but I believe that a little bit of it has to do with racism. Since that time, she's had custody battles. I don't know why. I could make excuses. I could try to figure out why she did it, but I don't know.

Although child abuse charges were filed against her mother, Kadija said that the legal system favored her mother. She stated, "Every single judge that we've had until this last one was a White male. They would always rule in her favor. All she had to do was cry in court and say 'I would never do that to my children.'" Kadija also admitted that on several occasions she lied in court to protect her mother, even though her mother had put her on a diet when she was eight years old that left her underweight and was present when the mother's second husband was sexually abusing Kadija. "At some point, her mind must have just snapped," Kadija said of her mother.

Despite the precariousness of her life during her elementary years, Kadija passed all her classes. She noticed differences between the two elementary schools that she attended and considered one to be superior to the other. Regarding the worse of the two schools, she stated, "I was still recovering from living with my mother. I do not believe that I got as much help as I needed. I got more help from home." Moreover, Kadija believed that most of the teachers at the better of the two schools cared about her but at the other school they did not. Although she believed that most teachers at both schools expected her to graduate from high school and become a successful adult, she was unsure of whether or not teachers at either school liked her personally.

During middle school, Kadija said that her bad attitude may have affected her relationships with her teachers, but she knew for certain that it had a definite effect on her relationship with her peers. She explained:

> I really don't think teachers got to know a whole lot of students. I don't know what it was with me in junior high. High school got a lot better. But junior high, I was just going through a phase. I just hated everyone and everyone hated me. It was bad. I mean I got good grades and everything. I was an average student .
>
> At the time, I had two really big enemies. One was a boy and one was a girl and she and I were just constantly at each other. We hated each other to the max because we thought we were copying off of each other. At the end of eighth grade, she invited me to her graduation party. I was not very involved with her crew, her group. I was just kind of like the tag along. I really didn't like these people.
>
> Ninth grade came around and she became my best friend. I think it was because we noticed that we were not just copying off of each other; it was that we were like each other. I think that has to do with maturity because now, I consider her my sister. She doesn't hang around with anyone of her old crew, except for one person. She was like my worst enemy but now she's my best friend.

In spite of the fact that Kadija was unsure whether or not most of her middle school teachers cared about her or even liked her, she felt that the quality of instruction provided by most was "good." Moreover, she believed that most of her middle school teachers expected her to graduate from high school and become a successful adult. Although her family problems persisted, Kadija was able to pass all her middle school courses.

In some ways, her high school years were an improvement over previous school years, but in other ways they were not. Although her interpersonal relationships improved at school, her family problems continued. Moving twice had caused her to attend two different high schools. Moreover, her father had been diagnosed with a rare and incurable disease that was slowly killing him. "He has lost feeling in one leg," she said. "He just had surgery on his eye. He had three tubes coming out of his chest. He takes several medications every morning. He's in constant pain."

Like her father, Kadija was also in constant pain, an emotional pain resulting in depression. Her father's refusal to sign the papers that were necessary for her to get professional counseling prevented her from benefitting from ongoing psychological assistance. In spite of this, Kadija decided to get a job while in high school. The result was that her grades went down. She also failed a Spanish course during her senior year. At the time of her interview, she had quit her job and was trying to improve her grades.

Kadija accepted sole responsibility for her poor high school grades and believed that the quality of instruction provided by most of her high school teachers, as well as most of her high school course work and homework, were "good." She thought that most of her high school teachers liked her, cared about her, expected her to graduate, and expected her to become a successful adult.

Three teachers stood out in her mind as exemplary high school teachers. Her tenth grade English teacher was outstanding in her opinion because "he was the one that got me to realize that I have more imagination than I thought. I've written one script but it got rejected. They told me that it was good but it was late in the season and they already had a similar idea. They also told me I needed an agent. I'm still working on a novel right now. My English teacher was the one who started me writing." Two ROTC instructors were among her best teachers because "they've been kind of like the listening ear. They were the ones who got me really interested in the military." Unlike most of the students who participated in the interview phase of the current study, Kadija said that she didn't have a "worst" high school teacher. "I've had some that I disliked but I never had one that when it comes to academics, they were the worst," she stated. "I just don't think I ever really understood them as well as some students did. That's all." In spite of the fact that she feared that her chronic depression, which she considered to be a major medical condition, might prevent her from joining the military or attaining a career in law enforcement, Kadija was optimistic about her backup plan to attend a local four-year university.

SUMMARY

Several narratives that have been presented thus far have described the high school experiences of some of the interviewees. Whereas some students found high school to be a positive experience, others found it to be problematic. Most interviewees said that they experienced a major problem or obstacle during their high school years. Kadija's narrative provides a detailed look at some of the problems that compounded the schooling experiences of one student. As with all the narratives that have been presented throughout this book thus far, this student refused to let her problems destroy her dreams. In fact, she experienced poverty, custody battles, abuse, continuous moving, and untreated depression, yet she still passed most of her elementary and secondary school classes. Therefore, a recurring theme that can be gleaned from most of the narratives is that many African American students are resilient enough to become stronger, instead of weaker, as a result of problems. Nevertheless, there is clearly a need for educators to become aware and more sensitive to some of the unique needs that adolescents who come from problematic backgrounds might have during their high school years.

Because ninth grade is a difficult period of adjustment for many students, additional precautions should be taken throughout the entire school year to assist students in acclimating to high school. In addition to offering before- and after-school assistance to students who are struggling academically, schools should also provide on-site counseling services for students, like Kadija, whose parents may not be willing to contact an outside health care provider. In most secondary schools, counselors spend the bulk of their time creating course schedules. Moreover, most school counselors are not trained to provide the psychological counseling that would serve the needs of students like Kadija. For these reasons, a different type of counselor—one who is trained in psychology or social work—is needed in schools.

9

High School Teachers

BEST HIGH SCHOOL TEACHERS

Whereas 33 percent of the students who completed the questionnaire said that they had two or more teachers who would qualify as their "best" elementary school teachers and 38 percent said that they had two or more "best" middle school teachers, 50 percent said that they had two or more "best" high school teachers. A few, however, said none would qualify as being the "best."

Nearly 60 percent of the students said that an English teacher was their "best" high school teacher, compared to 53 percent who said that a middle school English teacher was their "best." Forty-four percent of the students said that a math or history teacher was the "best." Students were least likely to select teachers who taught elective classes as their "best" teachers. Table 9-1 provides more information. Recurring themes were that the "best" teachers were patient, made learning fun, challenged students, gave extra help, had positive attitudes, and appeared to genuinely care about students.

A student who took college preparatory classes said that his eleventh grade business teacher "was the nicest teacher I've ever known. He could've had a bad day, but man he was nice." A G.A.T.E. student said that his eleventh grade English teacher was "by far the best teacher I ever had. He got me thinking in a different way after my stepdad's death and he even changed his lesson plans for me."

Another boy said that his tenth grade college preparatory English teacher was the "best" because "she wouldn't let me settle for less. She pushed me and she helped me and made sure that I got things done."

TABLE 9-1
Best High School Teachers

Course	Percentage of Students
1. Math	44
2. English	59
3. Science	37
4. Government	34
5. History	44
6. P.E.	21
7. Business	9
8. Shop	5
9. Drivers' Ed	17
10. Foreign Language	23
11. Music/Band	6

Note: The percentage total exceeds 100, because many students cited more than one teacher.

One girl explained that her eleventh grade American Literature teacher was the "best" because "she was fun. Even though we had to read a lot, she made projects. She was more of a friend than just a teacher. We could talk to her about anything." A girl who voluntarily left the G.A.T.E. program said that her eleventh grade English teacher was the "best" because "he goes out of his way for me. He connects with us and talks to us at our level." A student who took college preparatory high school courses said that his ninth grade math teacher was the "best" because he "showed lots of methods." A football player, who had three "best" teachers, said that his tenth grade P.E. teacher was an African American who "made me believe that I could do anything." His eleventh grade football coach "was cool and he gave me the impression that there was nothing that I couldn't do. The sky's the limit." His twelfth grade English teacher was one of the "best" because "he's smart; he teaches a lot. He uses vocabulary that I didn't even know existed. He puts it on the board and he explains it." Another student said that her twelfth grade government teacher was the "best" because "the work isn't boring, he had great guest speakers, and he wanted us to succeed."

A girl said that her American History teacher was the "best" because he "jokes, but doesn't let you get away with anything. He's encouraging and he taught me to be responsible." A boy who was enrolled in college preparatory classes during high school explained why his Algebra II teacher was the "best." "I'll mess up or miss a test and she's there after school. She helps anybody. If people don't understand, she'll stop and go back over it. If you don't understand something, you raise the red flag. If everybody raises the green flag, she'll go on. It really helps a lot because Algebra II is hard. On the first day of school, she gives everyone a red paper flag and a green one."

Another college preparatory student provided a detailed explanation of why her twelfth grade government teacher was the "best." "He's just a good teacher. He makes sure that we understand everything. He took his time to teach us. That was important. I think it's important to a lot of students that teachers take their time and really teach them. There's a difference between schooling and actually being taught something. It's important that the teachers actually teach and do their job." A boy who was in basic classes during high school said that he considered his ninth grade career teacher, who was also an advisor of an extracurricular club that he belonged to, the "best" because "he wants to make sure that everyone succeeds. He wants to take care of you. He'll go out of his way. His goal wasn't just to teach the subject he was teaching. His main goal was leadership and preparing you for the real world."

WORST HIGH SCHOOL TEACHERS

As with elementary and middle school, some students said that they did not have a "worst" high school teacher; others said that they had more than one that had earned this label. Twenty-four percent of the students who completed the questionnaire said that they had two or more teachers who would qualify as their "worst" high school teachers, versus 16 percent who said that they had more than one "worst" middle school teacher.

Forty-two percent of the students said that a math teacher was their "worst" high school teacher, compared to 38 percent who said that a math teacher was their "worst" middle school teacher. English and foreign language teachers were the second and third most commonly cited "worst" teachers (see Table 9-2). There was a low, but statistically significant, correlation between "worst" middle school teachers and "worst" high school teachers ($r = .23$; $p < .001$). Recurring themes were that the "worst" teachers did not appear to care about students, were impatient, mean, or boring.

A college preparatory student said that her ninth grade English teacher was the "worst" because "he was boring, and I didn't like the way he graded. It was never good enough and it was just so hard." A girl said that her tenth grade science teacher was the "worst" because "he had a heavy accent and was hard to understand." One student said that his tenth grade U.S. History teacher was the "worst" because "she

TABLE 9-2
Worst High School Teachers

Course	Percentage of Students
1. Math	42
2. English	33
3. Science	21
4. Government	9
5. History	15
6. P.E.	9
7. Business	3
8. Shop	1
9. Drivers' Ed.	3
10. Foreign Language	25
11. Music/Band	2

Note: The percentage total exceeds 100, because many students cited more than one teacher.

loses work. She doesn't help. She does a lot for herself but she's not there for students." Another student said that his tenth grade math teacher was the "worst" because "He wasn't a bad person, but the way he taught was not good. He was paranoid about students. He talked about students behind their backs."

Another college preparatory student said that her ninth grade geography teacher was the "worst" because "he didn't care; everything was meaningless. I was trying to learn, but he had that kind of 'whatever' attitude and was grumpy at that." Another student said that she had five teachers that were so awful, each could qualify as the "worst." She explained, "I've had teachers with the attitude, 'I really don't care if you graduate' and I had one who was racist and rude." A college preparatory student said that her tenth grade English teacher was the "worst" because "she cursed when we were noisy, she couldn't spell, and she didn't have a teaching credential." A student who was the statistician for her school's wrestling team and the "Water Girl" for the football team said that her ninth grade algebra teacher was the "worst" because "she picked on the African Americans and Hispanics. She was rude and she picked on me, because I am African American and I am quiet." A boy described his tenth grade entrepreneurship teacher as the "worst" because "she made sure that she treated me differently from everyone else in the class. She tried to disrespect me. I give teachers the respect they give me."

The interviewees were asked several additional questions about their high school teachers. The results are presented next.

Did Students Think That Most of Their High School Teachers Cared About Them?

When asked whether or not they thought that most of their high school teachers cared about them, the majority of the interviewees said "Yes." The percentage, 61 percent, however, was lower than the percentage of students who believed that their elementary teachers cared about them. However, a higher percentage of students believed that their elementary and high school teachers versus middle school teachers cared about them (see Table 9-3). One student said that her high school teachers cared about her because "I'm not a disrespectful person. I respect every elder there is. So it's not like they would have problems with me or anything." Conversely, a girl who did not believe that most of her high school teachers cared about her said, "They couldn't care less. It makes me mad to even think about that. It's terrible!"

Did Students Think That Most of Their High School Teachers Liked Them?

The majority of interviewees believed that most of their high school teachers liked them. In comparison to the percentage of students who believed that their teachers cared about them, a higher percentage believed that most teachers liked them. Nevertheless, students were more likely to think that their middle school and elementary teachers versus high school teachers, respectively, liked them (see Table 9-3). One student felt that most of her high school teachers liked her because "I was outgoing and spoke my mind." A student who did not believe that most of his high school teachers liked him explained, "Some teachers act like you were bothering them or something."

TABLE 9-3
Students' Perceptions of Their Teachers' Expectations and Beliefs about Them (by % of Interviewees and School Level)

	Elementary Teachers	Middle School Teachers	High School Teachers
Did they care?	75	54	61
Did they like them?	82	85	71
Did they expect them to graduate?	86	75	89
Did they expect them to become successful adults?	75	71	79

N = 28

Did Students Think That Most of Their High School Teachers Believed That They Would Graduate from High School?

Nearly 90 percent of the interviewees believed that most of their high school teachers thought that they would graduate. This percentage was higher than for elementary and middle school. Students were least likely to believe that middle school versus elementary or high school teachers expected them to graduate (see Table 9-3).

Did Students Think That Most of Their High School Teachers Believed That They Would Become Successful Adults?

Nearly 80 percent of the interviewees said that most of their high school teachers believed that they would become successful adults. This percentage was higher than that for elementary and middle school teachers. Furthermore, students were less likely to believe that their middle school versus elementary or high school teachers expected them to become successful adults (see Table 9-3). One student said that most of her high school teachers expected her to become a successful adult because "when I sit down and talk to them, they know where I'm going. They know where I want to be." The following narrative provides a glimpse into the elementary and secondary schooling experiences of a G.A.T.E. student.

TISHA

Of all the interviewees who participated in the current study, Tisha was one of the most vocal. She had been in G.A.T.E. classes since elementary school and had plenty to share about her schooling experiences. Because her mother was an instructional aide, she received ongoing parental support for her schooling. "My parents were always there, pushing me," she stated. "Nothing could have hindered me, because my family was always there to make sure I did my work, even if I was sick." Just as they held Tisha to a high academic standard, her parents also held the educational system to a high standard. For this reason, after deeming the curriculum to be too easy for Tisha at one elementary school, they had her transferred to a school that had higher standards.

Nevertheless, although Tisha rated the quality of instruction provided by most of her teachers at the second elementary school as "good," in retrospect, she was not completely satisfied with most of her elementary teachers. They appeared to like her personally and seemed to expect her to graduate and to become a successful adult, yet she believed that they really did not care about her.

She held the same viewpoint of most of her teachers at the prestigious public college-preparatory middle school that she attended. The overall quality of instruction was "good," the teachers appeared to like her and expected her to graduate and to become a successful adult, but they did not really seem to care about her. Despite this, she said that she had three "best" middle school teachers. Each of these teachers took a personal interest in her and challenged her.

During sixth grade, a year when Tisha had difficulty adjusting to middle school, a math teacher stood out as her "best" teacher. "She was one of those people that understands that you have family problems and other activities," Tisha explained, "but when it comes to school, you do your school work. If you had a problem, you would go to her desk and she would explain things. She didn't say, 'Ask your buddy; ask the person in the group,' because they're as clueless as you are." Tisha considered her seventh grade English teacher to be outstanding because "she knew what I needed, even though I thought I knew everything. She called my mom. She was just pushing me all of the time." Tisha, a flutist, made similar remarks about her eighth grade band teacher. "We had personal conflicts," she said, "but she pushed me and kept encouraging me."

Whereas Tisha had three outstanding middle school teachers, her seventh grade math teacher stood out as "worst" of all the rest. She recalled,

> He wasn't teaching math. He was just talking about his life, his personal problems. I can't remember if he got fired or if he moved to another school but he was no longer there by the time I got to eighth grade. He was just terrible. If you didn't like what he was saying, he would get so upset with you, but if you just sat there and laughed and acted like you really enjoyed him—doing that fake stuff—he was just like your buddy. I hated that. I mean teach something! Let me learn something! Don't let me learn about cars or how you can't stand your ex-wife. I don't think it should be a personal matter unless it's educational. Once he told me that I was just making excuses just like all of the Black people on Welfare.

Regarding homework and course work during her middle school years, Tisha also had mixed views. She believed that the course work was "beneficial" but the homework was not. "It was terrible!" she exclaimed. "They gave too much. There should be a balance."

Tisha reserved her most heated comments for her description of her high school years. It was during this period that she became aware of how tracking contributes to inequality of educational opportunity. She recounted, "I was in college prep classes and Honors classes. I looked at both perspectives. In the college prep classes, during my freshman year, if you showed up, you got a good grade. To me, in Honors classes they push you more. There shouldn't be a difference. All students should have the same education as Honors kids because it pushes them to do more."

Although she rated the overall quality of instruction that most of her high school teachers provided as "good," once again Tisha had mixed sentiments about other questions pertaining to her teachers. Whereas she believed that most of them liked her and expected her to graduate, she did not believe that they cared about her or expected her to become a successful adult. She stated,

> You could tell that they judge people by their race, by the color of their skin or background. We have a large amount of females who are pregnant at our school. The teachers look at you like you'll never be anything. I understand that the girls are responsible, but it also depends on the teachers. If the teachers look at you like you're not going to be anything, if they automatically assume that you're going to get pregnant, or you're going to get killed, or you're going to drop out, they're not really going to put that time or effort into you, because you're not going to be here next year. If teachers just show that they're really interested and that students need to go to school, it's more encouraging to people.

Just as she sensed that many teachers were biased against certain students who appeared to be doomed to failure, Tisha also noticed a similar bias from them toward herself. "When they heard that I was going to go to a community college, because transferring to a four year university is so low, they automatically assumed that I wouldn't get that far," she said.

One high school teacher, however, stood out above the rest. Tisha had her for her sophomore and senior years. This teacher taught American History and Advanced Placement Government. In describing her attributes, Tisha stated, "Even though she played around, she doesn't let you get away with anything. She even gave me a recommendation and I was surprised, because I only had a C in her class. I wasn't pushing myself like I should have and she knew that. She would ask me for my homework and I would say it was at home. She would say, 'Well, leaving it at home is not going to get you anywhere. You need to do what you need to do.'"

Tisha said that her "worst" high school teacher taught chemistry, the only course that she ever failed. She felt that he was not a good teacher because he made assumptions about students and had low expectations. "Freshmen year, I had a B in his class, the highest of everyone,"

Tisha stated. "And that's a shame, that I had the highest grade and it was a B. We didn't click, because I was a talker. I talked constantly and that was only in his class. I knew everything. I wasn't really paying attention. I knew the subject. He was using the same book we used in junior high. It wasn't really a challenge."

Tisha also criticized some of the course work and the homework practices at her high school. During freshman year, none of her college preparatory classes were "beneficial," except for math. "The work was too easy," she said. Her tenth, eleventh, and twelfth grade course work was "beneficial" because she was in Honors classes, which were more challenging. However, Tisha was totally dissatisfied with the homework policies of most of her teachers. "I didn't really get any homework, except during my sophomore and senior year," she stated.

In spite of her frustration with many of her schooling experiences, Tisha's goal was to become an elementary teacher. Furthermore, she refused to be dissuaded from attending a community college instead of a four-year university first, in spite of what her teachers said. Moreover, she was determined to show them that she would indeed succeed, even if they expected her to fail.

SUMMARY

This chapter yielded several noteworthy patterns regarding the students' secondary school years. For example, for both middle school and high school, the majority of "best" teachers taught English/language arts classes. Second, for both middle school and high school, math teachers were more likely than others to be considered the "worst." The students' comments revealed that "best" teachers wanted students to succeed, went out of their way to be helpful, had high expectations, pushed students to excel, and made the course work fun and interesting. "Worst" teachers had bad attitudes, appeared to single out certain students for unfair treatment, did not appear to care whether or not students succeeded, and refused to provide extra help. Additionally, in this chapter, more than any other previous chapter, perceptions of racism and racist practices surfaced. "Racism in school" is discussed in detail in chapter 12.

Another pattern that emerged was that whereas most of the interviewees believed that the majority of their elementary, middle school, and high school teachers cared about them, liked them, expected them to graduate, and expected them to become successful adults, there were differences according to students' level of schooling. For example, the interviewees were more likely to believe that their elementary and high school teachers versus middle school teachers cared about them, expected them to graduate, and expected them to become successful adults. On the other hand, the interviewees were more likely to think that their elementary and middle school versus high school teachers liked them personally.

Several possibilities might explain why the interviewees appeared to have a more negative view of their middle school teachers than others. One possibility is that students' developmental changes and unique needs during middle school might have clouded their perspective of their middle school teachers. Another possibility is that just as a high percentage of middle school teachers are underqualified to teach in their subject area, middle school teachers might be more likely than others to lack the interpersonal skills that adolescents in this age group need.

Two other themes that resurfaced in this chapter are the effects of tracking on students' schooling experiences and the effects of teacher attitudes and expectations. For example, Tisha's story illustrated some differences between college preparatory and Honors tracks. She noticed that in her freshman college preparatory classes, teachers practiced grade inflation and had lower expectations than what she was used to. One result was that Tisha, like many African American students, expressed boredom through excessive talking in class. Thereafter, she was perceived to be a discipline problem by at least one teacher. Moreover, because she decided to go to a two-, instead of four-year university first, she sensed that teachers stereotyped her. She also noticed that teachers had low expectations of certain students whom they believed would eventually drop out of school. These low expectations had a negative effect on teaching practices.

Finally, because half the students said that they had two or more "best" high school teachers, which was higher than the percentage who did for elementary or middle school, a logical conclusion is that just as high school denotes a beginning and an ending for many students, it can also signify an important turning point for students. For this reason it is important for high school teachers to be willing to invest as much time and effort in students as possible.

10

High School Course Work and Homework

COURSES THAT STUDENTS FAILED

The 271 students who completed the questionnaire answered several questions about their high school course work and homework. Whereas 15 percent of the students failed one or more middle school courses, nearly four times as many, 57 percent, said that they failed at least one high school course. Moreover, 34 percent of the students failed more than one high school course. Twenty-four percent failed two courses, 13 percent failed three, and 5 percent failed four high school courses. Nearly half the students who participated in the study failed a math course. Students were least likely to fail an elective course. Table 10-1 gives more information about the courses that students failed.

MOST DIFFICULT HIGH SCHOOL COURSES

Math was the "most difficult" high school subject for 70 percent of the students. Nearly 40 percent of the students said that a foreign language class was the "most difficult." English and science were the third and fourth most frequently cited "most difficult" courses. Table 10-2 provides more information about students' answers to this question.

EASIEST HIGH SCHOOL COURSES

More than half the students who completed the questionnaire said that P.E. or English was their "easiest" high school course. Students were less likely to say that math, science, foreign language, or government were their "easiest" core courses. Table 10-3 provides more information about students' responses.

TABLE 10-1
High School Courses That Students Failed

Course	Percentage of Students
1. Math	46
2. English	31
3. Science	23
4. Government	7
5. History	15
6. P.E.	6
7. Business	1
8. Shop	2
9. Drivers' Ed.	3
10. Foreign Language	17
11. Music/Band	1

N = 271

Note: The percentage total exceeds 100, because many students failed more than one course.

THE OVERALL QUALITY OF INSTRUCTION PROVIDED BY HIGH SCHOOL TEACHERS

Students who completed the questionnaire answered six questions about the overall quality of instruction that their high school teachers provided. The majority of students gave a high rating to the quality of instruction that most of their ninth grade teachers provided, but nearly

TABLE 10-2
The Most Difficult High School Courses

Course	Percentage of Students
1. Math	70
2. English	32
3. Science	31
4. Government	18
5. History	21
6. P.E.	3
7. Business	3
8. Shop	4
9. Drivers' Ed.	1
10. Foreign Language	38
11. Music/Band	1

N = 271

Note: The percentage total exceeds 100, because many students selected more than one course.

TABLE 10-3
The Easiest High School Courses

Course	Percentage of Students
1. Math	27
2. English	51
3. Science	29
4. Government	29
5. History	36
6. P.E.	63
7. Business	14
8. Shop	7
9. Drivers' Ed.	39
10. Foreign Language	23
11. Music/Band	0

N = 271

Note: The percentage total exceeds 100, because many students identified more than one course.

40 percent gave it a lower rating. Nearly half the students who were retained during elementary school gave it a lower rating (see Table 10-4). There was a statistically significant correlation between students' high school grade point average and how they rated the quality of their ninth grade instruction ($r = .34$; $p < .02$).

With the exception of elementary Special Education students, the percentage of students in all groups who were pleased with the quality of instruction provided by their tenth grade teachers was higher than for ninth grade. However, a higher percentage of students who were in G.A.T.E. during elementary school rated it as "good" or "excellent," and a higher percentage of students who were retained or not in G.A.T.E. during elementary school rated it as "fair" or "poor" (see Table

TABLE 10-4
How Students Rated the Quality of Instruction Provided by Most of Their Ninth Grade Teachers (by % of Students, Retainees, and Elementary Track)

Elem. Group	Poor	Fair	Good	Excellent
Total Sample	6	32	45	15
Retainees	8	39	41	12
Special Ed.	0	36	55	9
Basic	7	32	42	16
G.A.T.E.	2	30	50	13

N = 271

10-5). There was a statistically significant correlation between the students' high school grade point average and how they rated the quality of their tenth grade instruction ($r = .33$; $p < .01$).

Regarding the quality of instruction provided by most of their eleventh grade teachers, the majority of students in all groups rated it as high. A higher percentage of students who were retained during elementary school or in G.A.T.E. than other groups rated it as "poor." The percentage of G.A.T.E. students who rated it as "good" or "excellent" was also noticeably lower than it was for tenth grade. Conversely, a higher percentage of students who were in Special Education or Basic classes during elementary school were happier with the quality of instruction that their eleventh grade teachers provided than that provided by their ninth and tenth grade teachers (see Table 10-6). There was a statistically significant correlation between how students rated the quality of their eleventh grade instruction and their high school grade point average ($r = .33$; $p < .01$).

As with lower high school grade levels, the majority of students in all groups rated the quality of instruction provided by most of their twelfth grade teachers as high, but there were differences according to the students' elementary tracks. For example, a higher percentage of students who were in Special Education versus other classes during elementary school rated it as "poor" or "fair." Moreover, a higher percentage of those who were in Special Education during elementary school seemed more satisfied with the quality of their eleventh grade versus twelfth grade instruction (see Table 10-7).

There was a small, but statistically significant correlation between students' high school academic track and how they rated the quality of instruction that they received during their first three years of high school. The correlation between high school academic track and how students rated the quality of instruction provided by most of their ninth grade teachers was $r = .16$; $p < .01$. For the quality of their tenth grade

TABLE 10-5

How Students Rated the Quality of Instruction Provided by Most of Their Tenth Grade Teachers (by % of Students, Retainees, and Elementary Track)

Elem. Group	Poor	Fair	Good	Excellent
Total Sample	4	24	54	15
Retainees	8	23	61	8
Special Ed.	9	27	55	9
Basic	5	27	51	15
G.A.T.E.	2	13	63	16

N = 271

TABLE 10-6
How Students Rated the Quality of Instruction Provided by Most of Their Eleventh Grade Teachers (by % of Students, Retainees, and Elementary Track)

Elem. Group	Poor	Fair	Good	Excellent
Total Sample	5	22	49	20
Retainees	8	23	50	19
Special Ed.	0	18	64	18
Basic	5	22	48	22
G.A.T.E.	7	21	50	16

N = 271

instruction and high school academic track the correlation was r =. 15; p < .02. For eleventh grade the correlation was r = .15; p < .01.

Concerning the overall quality of instruction provided by most of their high school teachers, about half the students rated the quality of instruction that most of their teachers provided as "good," and 13 percent rated it as "excellent." Twenty-eight percent rated it as "fair," and 4 percent rated it as "poor." A student who rated the quality of instruction that most of his high school teachers provided as "fair" said, "Some teachers care and some won't help you if you're having trouble. I have some that will help you and some that will go straight home after school and won't really help you." Another student said that he rated it as "fair" because "it could've been better. A few of my teachers seem like they don't care."

THE AMOUNT OF HOMEWORK THAT HIGH SCHOOL TEACHERS ASSIGNED

Most students received high school homework four or five times per week. A higher percentage of students who were retained during ele-

TABLE 10-7
How Students Rated the Quality of Instruction Provided by Most of Their Twelfth Grade Teachers (by % of Students, Retainees, and Elementary Track)

Elem. Group	Poor	Fair	Good	Excellent
Total Sample	2	15	48	30
Retainees	4	15	46	27
Special Ed.	9	27	27	36
Basic	1	15	49	30
G.A.T.E.	2	14	50	32

N = 271

mentary school than others received homework less than three times per week (see Table 10-8). There was a statistically significant correlation between students' high school track and the number of days per week that they received homework ($r = .37$; $p < .001$). There were also several other statistically significant correlations.

For example, there was a slight, but statistically significant, correlation between the students' high school grade point average and the number of days per week that they received homework ($r = .18$; $p < .003$). The number of days per week that students were assigned homework during high school was also correlated to how they rated the overall quality of their ninth ($r = .65$; $p < .001$), tenth ($r = .62$; $p < .001$), eleventh ($r = .61$; $p < .001$), and twelfth ($r = .51$; $p < .001$) grade instruction. There was also a statistically significant correlation between the number of days per week that students received homework and how they rated the overall quality of their high school instruction ($r = .55$; $p < .001$).

THE AMOUNT OF TIME THAT STUDENTS SPENT ON THEIR HIGH SCHOOL HOMEWORK

Approximately 60 percent of the students spent four hours per week or more on homework during high school. Conversely, during elementary school, only 27 percent of the students spent four or more hours per week on homework, and during middle school 49 percent did so. A higher percentage of students who were in G.A.T.E. versus other types of classes during elementary school spent eight or more hours per week on their high school homework. A higher percentage of elementary Special Education students spent less than four hours per week on high school homework (see Table 10-9). The amount of time that students spent on homework during high school was linked to a number of other variables.

TABLE 10-8
The Number of Days per Week That Students Received Homework during High School

	One	Two	Three	Four	Daily
Elem. Group			%		
Total Sample	2	4	13	14	64
Retainees	4	15	4	19	58
Special Ed.	0	9	9	18	64
Basic	2	4	14	14	64
G.A.T.E.	2	4	13	13	63

N = 271

TABLE 10-9
The Number of Hours per Week That Students Spent on Homework Assignments during High School (by % of Students and Their Elementary Group)

Elem. Group	1 or less	2–3	4–5	6–7	8–9	10 or more
Total Sample	11	23	26	10	10	16
Retainees	23	12	31	8	12	12
Special Ed.	27	27	18	18	0	9
Basic	11	24	27	10	10	12
G.A.T.E.	5	18	23	9	13	29

N = 271

For example, there was a small, but statistically significant, correlation between the amount of time spent on high school homework per week and high school grade point average (r = .16; p < .01). The amount of time spent on high school homework was also correlated to how students rated the quality of their high school instruction. The strongest statistically significant correlation was between the amount of time spent on high school homework and how students rated the quality of their ninth grade instruction (r = .57; p < .001). The amount of time spent on high school homework was also linked to how students rated the quality of instruction they received in tenth (r = .54; p < .001); eleventh (r = .53; p < .001); and twelfth grade (r = .43; p < .001); and the overall quality of their high school instruction (r = .48; p < .001). The strongest correlation, however, was between the number of days per week that students received homework and the amount of time that they spent on homework (r= .75; p< .01).

BENEFITS OF HIGH SCHOOL HOMEWORK

More than half of the students said that most of the homework that was assigned to them during high school was not very beneficial. Students who were retained or in Special Education classes during elementary school were less likely than students in other types of classes to rate most of their high school homework as "beneficial" (see Table 10-10). Compared to how they rated the value of their middle school homework, a higher percentage of students who were in Special Education or basic classes during elementary school rated their high school homework as "beneficial." Conversely, a higher percentage of students who were in G.A.T.E. classes during elementary school found their middle versus high school homework to be "beneficial."

TABLE 10-10
How Students Rated the Benefits of Their High School Homework (by %
of Students, Retainees, and Elementary Track)

Elem. Group	Not Beneficial	Somewhat Beneficial	Beneficial
Total Sample	7	44	44
Retainees	12	49	39
Special Ed.	9	55	36
Basic	6	45	45
G.A.T.E.	9	39	45

N = 271

The value that students placed on their high school homework was linked to several other factors. For example, there was a low, but statistically significant, correlation between how they rated the benefits of their homework and their high school grade point average (r = .28; p < .001). There was also a statistically significant relationship between how students rated the benefits of their high school homework and the amount of time that they spent on their high school homework (r = .46; p < .001). A stronger correlation existed between how students rated the benefits of their high school homework and the number of days per week that they received homework (r = .64; p <.001).

There were statistically significant correlations between how students perceived the benefits of their high school homework and how they rated the quality of instruction provided by their ninth (r = .49; p < .001); tenth (r = .46; p < .001); eleventh (r = .46; p < .001), and twelfth (r = .37; p < .001) grade teachers. How they rated the benefits of their high school homework was also related to how they rated the overall quality of their high school instruction (r = .41; p < .001).

The following narratives describe the elementary and secondary schooling experiences of two girls who were in G.A.T.E. during elementary school but ended up in lower tracks during high school for various reasons.

SHEMENA

At the time of her interview, Shemena was planning to major in sociology. She was so determined to attain this goal that she had already started taking classes at a local community college. Shemena had attended elementary school in another school district than the one in which she attended high school. She had positive memories of her elementary schooling and rated the quality of instruction as "excellent."

During middle school, Shemena continued to take G.A.T.E. classes but said that she had a difficult time adjusting because her parents' divorce "kind of messed me up a little. Everything started falling down." Consequently, Shemena failed her eighth grade English class. Nevertheless, she rated the quality of instruction as "good" because it prepared her for high school and she felt that most of her teachers had a positive viewpoint of her. Moreover, she could not think of one single "worst" middle school teacher.

During high school, the downhill spiral that started in middle school continued. She moved three times and attended three different schools. Her grades suffered, and she was dropped from the G.A.T.E. program during freshman year. During the period spanning ninth through eleventh grades, Shemena failed a total of six classes—three English and three math classes. However, she eventually made them up during summer school.

Shemena's overall impression of her high school years was negative. She was unsure of whether or not the course work was "beneficial" but was certain that the homework was a waste of time. Therefore, she rated the quality of instruction provided by most of her teachers as "poor," saying, "I don't think I've learned what I should've learned. I don't have really good study habits. I had to learn on my own." She also felt that her teachers viewed her negatively and had low expectations of her. "They always thought that I was an academic disappointment," she stated. "They used to tell me that I was not going to be anything in life."

The "worst" teacher in her opinion was her American Literature teacher, whom she had during her junior year. "He would never help me," she said. "He always had an attitude problem. He would make me sit in the back of the classroom and get mad if I asked to move to the front to see the board." Conversely, the one teacher who Shemena considered to be her "best" high school teacher treated her differently. Shemena had this teacher for an eleventh and twelfth grade physical therapist class. "He was really nice and patient," she explained. "Now, I'm in an advanced class for trainers and we go to other schools to train students. We show them how to wrap, pace, and all that. He really helps us learn things." The enthusiasm that Shemena expressed when describing what she had learned from this teacher also surfaced when she discussed her future plans. In spite of the fact that she had a dim view of her high school experiences, she expected to continue her education in order "to become successful."

KERVIONA

Like Shemena, Kerviona was placed in the G.A.T.E. program during elementary school but started faltering academically during middle school. She also had mostly positive memories of her elementary school years and rated the quality of instruction as "good." "I learned a lot there," she stated. "I had a personal relationship with most of my teachers. They actually encouraged me." But her viewpoint of middle school was different.

Although she rated the overall quality of instruction that most of her middle school teachers provided as "good," Kerviona sensed that they did not really care about her. "They basically just gave the work and your grade," she explained. "Some really didn't like for you to ask questions. It was weird. They always wanted us to come in after school."

In high school, instead of G.A.T.E. classes, Kerviona was placed in lower-level college preparatory classes. Although she rated the quality of instruction as "good," Kerviona felt that many of her teachers "gave busy work." She stated, "Busy work is when they say, 'Read the chapter and get different questions from there,' and when we ask when to turn it in, they tell us that we were noisy, but we don't have to turn it in."

Kerviona, who was one of the few interviewees to say that she never had a "worst" high school teacher, believed that most of her teachers had positive beliefs and expectations of her. Her "best" high school teacher taught psychology. "I've known him since third grade," she stated. "He really cares. He is so wonderful. He doesn't get paid for being a student advisor, but he is really there to help you with anything."

In spite of the fact that two individuals who were close to her died during her high school years and her mom moved to another state, Kerviona kept her grades up. "It was kind of hard for me to concentrate in classes," she said, "but I eventually got over that." After earning a "D" in one course, however, she decided to repeat the course in order to earn a higher grade.

This determination also was evident when she discussed her future. "I have 13 brothers and sisters," she said. "I'll be the first to actually go to college and everyone has always encouraged me. I really have a passion for the medical field. I don't want to leave school without a degree. I'm really going for my master's. It's something that I really want to do to help my family members out," she explained" At the time of her interview, Kerviona was one step closer to attaining her dream of becoming a hospital administrator. She had already been accepted to a four-year private university.

SUMMARY

This chapter presented feedback from students regarding high school course failure, course difficulty, the overall quality of instruction provided by their high school teachers, and additional feedback about their high school homework. Nearly four times as many students failed at least one high school course than failed a middle school course. Moreover, many students failed more than one high school course.

Again, math surfaced as problematic for numerous students. Nearly half the students who completed the questionnaire failed a high school math course. Furthermore, 70 percent said that math was their "most difficult" high school subject. As for many students during middle school, English/language arts, however, was identified as the "easiest" high school core subject for slightly more than half the students.

When asked to rate the quality of instruction that they received for each grade level, differences surfaced. Students felt that the quality of instruction that they received in the upper high school grades was better than that of the lower high school grades. Twice as many students rated the quality of instruction that they received during twelfth grade as "excellent" compared to what they received in ninth grade, and twice as many rated the quality of their ninth grade as "fair" compared to their twelfth grade instruction. This is extremely important because the students attended high school in a region that has a high ninth grade dropout rate. Therefore, one variable that might contribute to the high ninth grade dropout rate is the quality of instruction that many students receive during ninth grade.

Students' elementary track also had some bearing on how they rated the quality of instruction provided by their high school teachers. Those who were in G.A.T.E. during elementary school were more likely than those who were retained or in Special Education classes to be satisfied with the quality of instruction that they received. Other differences also indicated that students' elementary track had some bearing on their perception of the quality of their schooling experiences.

More than half of the students said that their high school homework was not very beneficial, yet homework and several other variables were correlated in a statistically significant manner. Students who were retained or in Special Education classes during elementary school were less likely than others to find their homework "beneficial." However, most students who were in either Special Education or basic classes during elementary school were more satisfied with their high school homework than middle school homework. Students who were in G.A.T.E. during elementary, on the other hand, were more likely to be pleased with their middle school versus high school homework.

Students who rated their high school homework as "beneficial" were more likely to have a higher grade point average than those who did not. They were also more likely to spend more time on their homework and feel satisfied with the quality of instruction provided by their high school teachers.

Part IV

Other Issues

11

Attitudes about College and Future Plans

As recently as 1959, more than half the Black families in the United States lived below the poverty level. By 1998, the number had decreased to 25 percent (National Center for Education Statistics, 1999). Although a disproportionately high percentage of African Americans still live in poverty, the percentage of African Americans who are considered "middle class" has grown substantially over time. One of the main reasons for these socioeconomic improvements is that the educational attainment of African Americans has also increased. Since 1976, the percentage of Black high school graduates enrolled in college has increased significantly (*Digest of Education Statistics* 2000). Several themes have surfaced regarding the factors that are most likely to determine college attendance among African Americans.

Two recurring themes are that students' academic track and the types of courses that they take in high school are predictors of whether or not they will attend college. Wilson and Allen (1987) studied 201 young African American adults in order to clarify the relationship between family practices and educational attainment. They found that for the subjects that they studied, the pattern of courses taken in high school was the best predictor of educational attainment. The subjects' parental status was the next greatest predictor, followed by their age, and whether or not their high school counselors had been helpful in encouraging them to attend college. The subjects' mothers' level of educational attainment was the next strongest predictor.

Burdman (2000) stressed the relationship between taking Advanced Placement (AP) courses in high school and college attendance. AP courses are supposed to be more rigorous than others. Therefore, students who take AP courses are rewarded with extra credit and a level of prestige, indicating that they can handle college work. Unfortunately, African American and Hispanic students have traditionally been under-represented in AP classes. For this reason the American Civil Liberties Union (ACLU) has filed a lawsuit on behalf of African American and Hispanic students who have been denied access to AP classes. The lawsuit alleges that schools that are dominated by White students are more likely than predominantly Black and/or Hispanic schools to offer students a wide selection of AP classes (Dupuis, 1999).

Another theme that has constantly surfaced in the literature regard-ing factors affecting college attendance rates and success in college of minority students is the quality of math preparation that they received. Drew (1996), as noted previously, described numerous reasons why students of color continue to receive inadequate math preparation for college. Among them are underprepared teachers, low teacher expecta-tions, and ineffective instructional practices. He concluded that inade-quate math and science preparation not only affects college attendance but also widens the economic gap between the poor and those from higher socioeconomic groups.

Polite (1999), as noted previously, conducted a study involving Afri-can American male high school students. The students believed that counselors and teachers, particularly math teachers, had shortchanged them academically through apathy and a nonchallenging curriculum. Later, these students had difficulty in college. Polite concluded that these students' experiences mirrored that of many African Americans nationwide.

The region in which the students who participated in the current study resided has one of California's lowest college attendance rates. For example, in 1990, 30 percent of the state's high school graduates age 25 and over had graduated from college. In the county in which the study's participants resided, however, only 20 percent of high school graduates age 25 and over had graduated from college (U.S. Census Bureau, 2000). The students who participated in the interview phase of the current study were asked several questions about college and their future plans. The total sample of 271 students were asked for recom-mendations regarding how the public school system can better prepare students for college. The results are presented in this chapter.

FUTURE PLANS

Ninety-six percent of the students who were interviewed said that they planned to attend college. Most stated that they wanted to improve their socioeconomic status. However, at the time when the interviews took place, only 68 percent of the African American high school seniors who were interviewed had actually applied to college. Students who were in high school Honors or college preparatory classes were more likely than others to have already applied for college at the time of their interview. In explaining why college was important to her, one girl who had already applied to a community college stated,

> I feel like high school is good and everything, but it's not going to get you far. I don't want to be at a nine or ten dollar job when I'm 25 years old. I feel if I had a B.A. or A.A., I'd be able to pursue becoming a Deputy Coroner, making like $50,000 to $60,000 a year, probably more than that. I really don't know, but a high school diploma won't get you where you wanna go money wise, your house, all that.
>
> I like helping people. A Deputy Coroner is interesting because, it's like death happens everyday. People get murdered and killed. I wanna know what it's like. It's interesting to me. It may be hard for me to do at first, like going out to the crime scene or whatever, but I'll get used to it. When I was in junior high, I was always interested in law. I wanted to be a lawyer. When I got to tenth grade, we had a guest speaker. What she was saying was really interesting. I wanted to know more about it, so she gave me this list of schools where I can get the classes that I need.

Several students explained that although they planned to eventually go to college, they had not applied because they were planning to go into the military first.

One student, a football player, said that even though many colleges had contacted him, he planned to attend a community college first, instead of a four-year university, because he was unaware of how to go about applying. He stated, "I didn't apply to a four year because I didn't really know about applying or anything. I was just getting letters and everything, but none of them said anything about how to apply. I have a box full of letters to play football. I didn't know until a couple of months ago [how to apply] and it was too late because the scholarship deadline was like December or January."

PREPARATION FOR COLLEGE

The interviewees were also asked whether or not their school district had adequately prepared them for college. Sixty-four percent said "Yes," and nearly 30 percent said "No." Some students said that the school district had done its job but students needed to become more responsible. One student said that she felt adequately prepared for college because her high school had a better reputation than other high schools in the same district. Another student stated, "I took the time to get the help and they were there to give me the help." One girl said that Honors students get adequate preparation for college but college preparatory students get less preparation. Another girl felt that her teachers had provided her with good study habits.

Conversely, those who felt that they were not adequately prepared tended to criticize the quality and lack of rigor of the curriculum, their lack of preparation for standardized tests, and the quality of instruction provided by some of their teachers. Several students even referred to the work that they were required to do as merely "baby work." This has repeatedly surfaced in previous chapters. One boy said his district had not prepared him for college, because he was "disgusted" by his standardized test scores. A girl who was in G.A.T.E. classes during elementary and middle school said that some aspects of the curriculum did not match what she felt she needed to know for college or what the SAT covered. She explained:

> I know our school has an agenda to follow, things they have to teach us but there are certain things we don't need to know. In English, we're learning about British literature and different things. I went and took the SAT. I thought, you know, I took English. I've aced it all four years and I think that I'm gonna do okay on the SAT. I get to the SAT and it's nothing that I've ever learned in school. It's like what are they preparing me for? I didn't know anything. I felt so dumb, but I passed good enough to get in college.

Another student said that only two of his classes, an economics class and an English class, had prepared him for college. He stated:

> Teachers should get us motivated because a lot of us are just turned off by the work we do in class. A lot of people get too bored and they will just fall asleep in class, fly off into space, or they'll just go do something else. That's why a lot of teachers have problems because they can't keep our minds motivated. If they could just do that, then maybe we could get more work done and do even better on tests.

ENCOURAGEMENT FROM OTHERS ABOUT COLLEGE

The interviewees were also asked whether or not their relatives, teachers, and school counselors had encouraged them to go to college. Ninety-three percent said that at least one of their teachers had encouraged them to attend college, and 93 percent said that at least one of their relatives had done so. Eighty-six percent said that a counselor had encouraged them to go to college. On the other hand, only 68 percent said that an adult at school had actually told them how to apply for college or when the deadlines were.

Consequently, 32 percent of the interviewees rated the quality of service provided by their high school counselors as "poor." Recurring themes from the students who were dissatisfied with the quality of service provided by their high school counselors were (1) Counselors failed to tell them crucial information regarding graduation requirements early enough, and (2) Counselors failed to tell them crucial information about applying to college.

Regarding the quality of service provided by his high school counselors, a boy who was in G.A.T.E. during high school said, "It's terrible. They're not involved at all. There's no contact, nothing at all! I had to do all my college stuff on my own." Another boy said that his counselor "didn't even tell me to go to a four year. She wouldn't say nothing." A third boy stated, "My counselor really hasn't been helping me out. She just gives me my schedule and lets me know if I'm going to fail a class or something." One girl said that her counselor "used to tell me that I wasn't going to be able to graduate and be who I wanted to be. A counselor is supposed to be there for you." Another girl said that counselors "don't help you get ready for college. You have to do it on your own. I tried talking to a counselor and she said, 'Well, we understand that the best thing for you to do is to get into a community college.' That's what they try to throw at me, but if I did all four years here, I'm not tryin' to go to nobody's community college." Another girl made similar comments, explaining that "my counselor was telling me that it would be cheaper for me to go to a community college first, because most kids that go to a university drop out or it's too hard for them and they end up going to a community college. He said that a community college will prepare me for the university."

Conversely, students who rated the quality of service that their counselors provided as "excellent," "good," or "fair" tended to place more responsibility on students versus counselors. One boy said that the quality of counseling that he received was "actually great. It depends upon you. If you really want to take care of business, it's on you to come in." A girl made similar remarks, stating, "My counselors were the type that said that if you want to find out something, then you go look for it. So it depends on who you are. So I would say [the quality of service] it's fair." However, at least one student who did take the initiative to seek information from his counselor was still somewhat dissatisfied with the quality of service he received. "I really didn't have an understanding of how to apply to college and I went to see my counselor to talk extensively to her more than once at the end of my eleventh grade year," he stated. "I wanted to understand but it took her that long to tell me how to apply to college."

RECOMMENDATIONS

The 271 African American students who completed the questionnaire were asked, "In your opinion, in what ways can the public school system better prepare students for college?" The interviewees were given an opportunity to address this question in detail.

Two recommendations were cited by more than half the 271 students who participated in the study. Sixty-one percent said that the public school system can better prepare students for college by teaching better study skills. Nearly 60 percent of the students said that more counseling about college is needed. The third most frequently cited recommendation, "Offer College Preparatory classes to all students," was recommended by nearly half the participants in the study.

Five suggestions were recommended by at least 40 percent of the 271 students. Forty-five percent urged educators to provide students with better math skills. The fifth most frequently cited recommendation was "hire better teachers." Students who were in G.A.T.E. classes during elementary school were more likely than other groups to make this suggestion and more than half did so. A substantial percentage of students also said that the quality of college preparatory classes should be improved. Again, those who were in G.A.T.E. during elementary school were more likely than others to make this recommendation. Forty-one percent of the students said that increasing parent involvement would be helpful in better preparing students for college. A considerable percentage of students also indicated that "more writing practice" is needed in order to better prepare students for college. Table 11-1 provides more information about the students' recommendations.

During the interview phase of the study, students' comments regarding how the school system can better prepare students for college tended to fit into one of four categories: provide more information and services related to college; offer more assistance in preparing students for the SAT and ACT; improve the curriculum; and allow more students to gain access to college preparatory classes.

Many students said that there should be before- and after-school programs that are aimed at providing all students with information about college, including how to apply for scholarships. Several students mentioned that although their schools were already providing some of the aforementioned information and services, only certain students were given access to these services. Some interviewees stressed that they wanted the opportunity to take field trips to colleges and hear guest speakers discuss the college experience. One girl, who ran track, complained that "only certain students get to go on the trips that they do have. I didn't get to go because I wasn't able to join any clubs because of athletics."

TABLE 11-1

How Public Schools Can Better Prepare Students for College (by % of Students Who Cited Each Recommendation and Their Elementary Group)

Recommendation	Total Sample	Elementary Group Retainees	Spec.Ed.	Basic	G.A.T.E
Teach Better Study Skills	61	50	27	63	59
More Counseling about College	58	54	46	60	55
Offer College Prep for All Students	48	35	27	51	41
Better Math Preparation	45	42	36	47	39
Hire Better Teachers	42	42	36	40	52
Improve College Prep Classes	41	31	36	40	45
Increase Parent Involvement	41	39	27	43	36
More Writing Practice	40	42	36	44	27
Better Critical Thinking Skills	34	35	18	36	34
Offer SAT/ACT Prep in Elem. School	29	19	18	28	34
More Reading Assignments	23	31	18	25	18
Offer College Prep in Elem. School	21	8	5	20	27
Assign More Homework	11	23	9	11	13

N = 271

Note: Percentage totals exceed 100, because students could make multiple recommendations.

Another message that was emphasized by many students was that they wanted a more challenging curriculum. Numerous students said that their course work was too easy, and several referred to it as "baby work" or "busy work." Moreover, 41 percent of the 271 students who completed the questionnaire that was used for the current study indicated that the quality of college preparatory classes should be improved. Students stated that they wanted course work that would truly prepare them to do college-level work. One girl said that teachers should "hold students more accountable and make them work." Another girl stated, "I think that some of the teachers are tryin' to get the students to like them, but if they toughen up, that will better prepare them. I have some teachers right now that are tryin' to be more our friends than our teachers. Teachers can still be cool with the students, but they need to toughen up." Another girl said that higher standards and holding students more accountable would benefit students "because in college you're not gonna have somebody there 24 hours a day telling you stuff." One student complained, "All of my classes I have right now are really easy and the teachers don't do anything. They don't have control over the classroom. They just talk and sit there. They don't even teach what they are supposed to be teaching." Another student summarized the sentiments of many interviewees by stating, "I think that instead of giving us a lot of busy work, they should have courses specifically designed like college courses, so we can better prepare ourselves to go into those courses. So, instead of giving us high school work, give us college work, so we'll know what to expect when we get there."

Many interviewees also underscored the need for schools to provide students with more assistance in preparing for the standardized tests that have been traditionally used as gatekeepers for college admission. Numerous students complained that their high school curriculum had nothing in common with what the standardized tests measured. Therefore, they felt totally unprepared. Nearly 30 percent of the 271 students said that this preparation should start as early as elementary school. Some interviewees said, however, that at the very least, it should start during ninth grade. Some students suggested that high schools should offer a special course that is designed to prepare students for these tests. Others said that this preparation should be incorporated into existing classes. For example, one student stated, "When we go take the SAT or ACT, some of the work on the ACT is similar to what we do in school. But on the SAT, it's different because we're not learning nothing from there and some of the words we don't understand. It's like we're lost."

Nearly half the 271 students said that all students should have the opportunity to take college preparatory courses, and 21 percent said that college preparatory classes should be offered as early as elementary school. Many of the interviewees were emphatic in their belief that every student should have access to courses that are designed to prepare students for college. One girl said that in addition to increasing the number of available college preparatory classes, "they should prepare students in regular classes for college too." Another exclaimed, "College Prep should be mandatory!"

SUMMARY

This chapter presented feedback from African American students regarding their future plans, particularly those about college. Nearly all the interviewees planned to attend college. The majority of interviewees also said that at least one relative, teacher, or school counselor had encouraged them to attend college. At the time of their interviews, however, only 68 percent had actually applied to any college or university. This is the same percentage of interviewees who said that an adult at school had told them how to apply for college and when the deadlines were. Therefore, it can be assumed that if more students had received formal advisement regarding the college application process, perhaps a higher percentage would have applied by the time of their interview. Moreover, about one third of the interviewees rated the quality of counseling services at their high school as "poor." Some students even stated that their counselors appeared to have low expectations of them and even advised them not to apply to four year-universities.

Although the majority of interviewees said that they planned to attend college, only 64 percent believed that their school district had actually prepared them for college. A recurring theme that has continuously surfaced from the narratives and other comments is that many students believed that they received a low level of instruction and were subjected to low teacher expectations. Some students complained that in addition to not being challenging, the curriculum failed to prepare them for standardized tests, and it was boring. Conversely, other students believed that the curriculum was sufficient but that students needed to accept more responsibility for preparing themselves for college. The fact that some counselors told students that four year univer sities were too difficult for them indicates that the counselors were aware that students were receiving a low level of instruction that had failed to adequately prepare them for four-year college/university course work or that the counselors believed that the students were not capable.

The total sample of students, those who completed the questionnaire, were asked for recommendations regarding how schools can better prepare students for college. "Teach better study skills" and "Provide more counseling about college" were recommended by the majority of students. Two issues regarding college preparatory classes also became evident: the lack of access to these classes and improving the curriculum. Nearly half the students said that all students should have an opportunity to take college preparatory classes. Again, this implies that many students are aware of the differential schooling experiences that students have according to their academic track. It also implies that African American students truly want to receive adequate preparation for college and they want access to academic tracks that are supposed to offer a more challenging curriculum. More than 40 percent of the students also stated that college preparatory classes should be improved. Again, a recurring theme has been that students are concerned that the curriculum is not as rigorous as it should be. In one of the previous narratives, a student contrasted her college preparatory and Honors classes and found the college preparatory classes to be woefully lacking in rigor and teacher expectations. Another student said that the boring and nonchallenging curriculum not only failed to hold students' attention, but it actually created discipline problems. This same message was conveyed through some of the narratives and students' comments in previous chapters.

"Provide better math preparation" was the fourth most frequently cited recommendation. This is extremely important for several reasons. First, it became clear that math surfaced as a challenging subject for many students at least starting in middle school, and for some even during elementary school. Second, the problem worsened during high school. Most students said that math was their most difficult high school subject, and the majority failed at least one high school math course. The students' recommendation clearly shows that they know that they need assistance with math and they want their teachers to provide a better math curriculum and better instructional practices that pertain to math. As noted in the characteristics of outstanding educators that students cited, math teachers need to do a better job of "explaining things well," "making the course work interesting," "giving extra help," and "being patient" with students. As also noted by students, "giving lots of homework" is not the answer. Students need meaningful homework that has a purpose. However, if they are already struggling with course work, giving them homework that they will not be able to complete on their own without assistance is counterproductive.

A substantial number of students also recommended that better teachers be hired. Most students who participated in the current study made numerous comments, either by writing additional comments on the questionnaire or during the interview phase of the study regarding effective versus ineffective teachers. A continuous message has been that students want teachers who are willing to form personal relationships with them. They want teachers who challenge them academically but who are also committed to helping students succeed. Too many students felt that certain teachers did not care whether or not students succeeded in their classes. Many students felt that discipline, versus learning, was the main focal point of some teachers. Given that many teachers, as noted several times throughout this book, are truly underprepared to teach the subjects that they teach and are lacking the interpersonal skills and instructional practices that would improve their relationships and success rates with African American students, this recommendation from students is particularly relevant.

More than 40 percent of the students also recommended that schools "increase parent involvement." This implies that African American students want schools to make more of an effort to invite their parents to become active participants in their schooling. Several narratives and other comments from students indicated that "best" teachers made an effort to contact parents or guardians. Chapter 14 addresses the issue of "parent involvement" in more detail.

12

Racism at School

Although the United States has prided itself on being the most democratic country in the world, racial tensions and hate crimes have been persistent problems throughout its history and continue today (Hacker, 1992; Manning & Baruth, 2000). Because schools are microcosms of the larger society, the same is true of schools (Delpit, 1995; Nieto, 2000; Poplin & Weeres, 1992). Shipler (1997) said that for many students, race/ethnicity starts to become a factor in peer selection during the middle school years and by high school, most friendships are based on race/ethnicity. In their study of four public schools, Poplin and Weeres (1992) concluded that race, culture, and class were connected to every theme that surfaced. Whereas many students of color viewed schools as being racist, however, some teachers disagreed with the students' perspective.

Despite its long history, racism is still a controversial topic in America. Although hate crimes continue to proliferate in the United States and other countries, such as Germany, France, and Israel, the topic evokes discomfort, avoidance, denial, or outrage for many Americans, including educators. One of the results of the proliferation of racism in the United States is that since the 1980s, there has been a greater division between African Americans and Whites on college campuses (Comer & Poussaint, 1992). However, racism and racial tensions are also prevalent on some precollege campuses.

In its "Schools and Staffing Survey" for 1990–91 and 1993–94, the *Digest of Education Statistics 1999* reported that the percentage of public school teachers who believed that racial tension was a serious problem at their school had increased over time. Furthermore, secondary teachers were more likely than elementary school teachers to report that it was a serious problem.

Children are not immune to either experiencing racism, perpetrating racism, or to the awareness that racism exists. Researchers have posited that for African American children, the notion of racism and the awareness that racism exists are inextricably tied to their emotional, cognitive, and social development. Wilson (1987) argued that African American children become aware of their ethnicity around age three and this awareness has a pronounced effect on their development and relationships with others, both within and outside of their own racial group. White and Parham (1990) said that African American children become aware of the existence of racism long before they are able to verbalize it. Regardless of when they become aware of it, this knowledge can have a detrimental effect on Black children. Among the negative outcomes that White and Parham cited are bitterness, fear, anger, and resentment. In her resiliency study, Thompson (1998) found that racism/discrimination was the most frequently cited problem that the African American college students experienced during childhood or adolescence and it had a moderate or strong effect on 94 percent of those who experienced it. The average student was 13 years old at the time when the incident(s) occurred.

Comer and Poussaint (1992) said that between ages 9 through 12, African American children's attitude about their own race and that of others tends to become fixed. The attitudes that are adopted stem from (a) the types of experiences related to race that children have had and (b) the messages about other racial/ethnic groups that they receive from their parents or primary caregivers. Moreover, being totally isolated from Whites or being totally isolated from African American culture can cause problems for Black and biracial youths. During adolescence, however, individuals tend to reevaluate their beliefs about racial issues. African American adolescents may adopt one of two stances regarding racism, according to Comer and Poussaint: They may feel hopeless about it or they may search for solutions.

McAdoo (1992) studied the ways in which middle-class Black families cope with adversity. She found that Black parents are forced to teach their children the "duality of Black existence." In other words, in addition to ordinary parenting responsibilities, they have to inculcate their children with strategies that will enable them to survive in two distinct arenas—one Black, the other White. McAdoo also stated that one of the most obvious differences between middle-class White and middle-class Black families is that the Black families are not only aware of racial oppression but have to develop strategies to deal with it. She concluded that Black children who are "overprotected" from stressors such as racism and negative peer influence have difficulty in coping later in life.

The middle-class Black families that she studied coped with racism in four primary ways: (1) through accepting the fact that racism transcended class; (2) through assimilation; (3) through embracing the church and the belief that the hereafter would be better than the present; and (4) through embracing Pan-Africanism and identifying with African, instead of Western, norms.

One of the most prevalent manifestations of racism that numerous African American children and adolescents experience is racism in the form of de facto segregation (Comer & Poussaint, 1992). Nearly five decades after the Supreme Court outlawed segregation in public school, countless schools throughout the nation continue to be segregated. Nieto (2000) differentiated among several types of racism that can be found in American schools. One form is segregation among schools, which results in schools that are predominated by children of color ending up with less funding than predominantly White schools. Another form of racism stems from tracking, which results in disproportionate numbers of African American and Hispanic students being placed in Special Education and lower-level tracks, instead of G. A.T.E. (Hacker, 1992; Oakes, 1999).

Moreover, as noted previously, another indicator of racism is that predominantly minority schools are more likely to have underprepared teachers and teachers who are teaching outside of their areas of expertise (Quality Counts, 2000; Wilson, 1996). Furthermore, as also noted previously, Au (1993) found that teachers who teach children from a lower socioeconomic status spend less time on literacy-building activities than other teachers. Another way in which racism manifests itself in schools is through low teacher expectations for children of color, which results in lower standards and a watered down curriculum (Au, 1993; Comer & Poussaint, 1992; and Hare & Hare, 1991). In an effort to provide educators with more information about race relations in schools, the African American students who participated in the current study were asked numerous questions about racism. The results are presented in this chapter.

RACISM AT SCHOOL: QUESTIONNAIRE RESULTS

Forty three percent of the 271 students who completed the questionnaire said that they had experienced racism at their high school. A higher percentage of students who were in the Special Education program during elementary school (55 percent) than those who were in Basic (40 percent) or G.A.T.E. (43 percent) classes said they had. Furthermore, there was a statistically significant correlation between grade retention during elementary school and experiencing racism during high school (r = .33; p < .001). Additionally, among the students who experienced racism at school, 45 percent said that it occurred "rarely," but more than half said that it occurred "occasionally" or "frequently."

Nearly 70 percent of the students who experienced racism at their high school said that the culprit was another student. Conversely, one third said that the culprit was an adult on campus. Moreover, 6 percent cited more than one source (see Table 12-1).

The majority of students (67 percent) who said that they experienced racism at their high school did not report it. Those who did report it were most likely to report it to a parent or another student. They were least likely to report it to an adult who worked at their school site.

Whereas 43 percent of the students said that they had personally experienced some form of racism at their high school, a higher percentage, nearly 60 percent, said that they knew at least one other student who had experienced racism at the same high school.

Students were also asked to rate the overall racial climate at their school. Nearly 70 percent said that racism exists at their high school but it is uncommon. Conversely, one fifth said that racism not only exists at their high school, but that it is common as well. Only 10 percent of the students said that racism does not exist at their high school.

ADDITIONAL INFORMATION FROM THE INTERVIEWEES

The students who participated in the interview phase of the study provided additional information about issues pertaining to racism at school. In addition to having an opportunity to elaborate on the racial climate at their high school, they were also given an opportunity to discuss the racial climate at their elementary and middle schools, and to describe specific racist incidents that they themselves may have perpetrated or to which they may have been subjected.

TABLE 12-1
The Culprit(s) of the Racism That Students Experienced at Their High Schools (by % of Students Citing Each Culprit)

Culprit	Total Sample
Other Student(s)	66
Staff	9
Teacher(s)	16
Administrator(s)	6

N = 117

The majority of the interviewees, 57 percent, said that they had personally experienced some form of racism at some point at school. Some also said that they were aware that other students, not only African Americans, but Whites and Latinos as well, had experienced racism at school. Furthermore, although most of the interviewees said that they experienced it at their high school site, a small percentage, 14 percent, said that it started during elementary school. For example, one biracial student said that he experienced racism at school frequently, starting in first grade. During this time, his peers excluded him by refusing to play with him, and often he was subjected to racial slurs. In chapter 1, Destiny, a biracial girl, also described her own early ongoing experiences with exclusion and harassment that were based on race.

Indeed, for most of the interviewees, racism surfaced through racial slurs that came from other students. For others, however, it surfaced through what students perceived to be unfair biased behavior on the part of teachers, staff members, or administrators. For example, students described instances of being singled out by school security but witnessed students of other races being treated more favorably.

As in some of the narratives and comments that were presented in previous chapters, several students, however, said that they had experienced racism from teachers. For example, a girl said that one of her teachers "wouldn't care. She would pick on you, single you out, or blame me for something I didn't do." Another student felt that a History teacher was racist for accusing her of cheating when she had not cheated on a test. One boy said that, in his opinion, racism is common at his school "because of the way some teachers treat students regarding grades." Another boy, who also believed that racism was common at his school, stated, "I've seen it. Throughout the whole school, other students, faculty members, and administrators have seen it. It's kind of sad." A girl said that she had a problem with a teacher during summer school. "I asked him for a tissue and he said, 'Do I look like your slave?' He was like, 'Oh, yeah, you should know something about that.' That's the only thing that I experienced."

Some incidents, however, resulted in physical altercations among students. One girl stated, "I remember in my ninth and tenth grade year, there were a lot of fights between Mexicans and Blacks, but now it's not as bad. It's still around but it's not as bad." Another student said that she witnessed race riots between Mexican and African American students at her school. In describing events that he perceived to be racist, one boy explained,

> One time when I was in seventh grade, my English teacher said, "You look like a chocolate brownie." She said it in front of the whole class and the class laughed. I laughed it off, but I thought about it and that's when it

kicked in. But I wasn't really hurt. I didn't tell my parents but I did tell them about the time a girl called me a nigger. She called me that because I accidentally bumped into her and I guess I didn't say "sorry." She got loud and I told her to "shut up" and she said "you stupid nigger," stuff like that. We got in a little fight.

I was in seventh grade, so I pushed her. Then, she tried to fight me, so I just threw her around the classroom. I never hit her. I just threw her. We had a substitute that day, so we went to the office and talked to the vice principal about it. He was telling me how I should handle myself and he let her know that she shouldn't be using those words. So it got resolved. Now, we're friends.

Several African American students said that they had learned to ignore signs of racism and had also learned to differentiate between "real" racism and "common" racism. It appeared that they had heard so many racial slurs that they had learned to ignore them. In their opinion, "real" racism was the "heavy duty" or more serious forms of racism. One student, who said that racism exists at her high school but it is uncommon, said, "There are rumors of Skinheads here, but I haven't seen any. I feel really comfortable here." Another student said, "My father told me, 'You're gonna find many people who don't like you because of your race or because of who you are. You gotta learn how to deal with it. Then, keep going.'"

Most of the interviewees said that they had never subjected another student to racism. However, one student, who said that she experienced racism occasionally in high school, said that her experiences at school had actually turned her into a racist. She explained:

My mom told me that if I let things like that get to me, then I need to be a stronger person, instead of letting what someone else says get to me, because they'll make me or break me. Like during a conversation, I'll hear Hispanic people saying, "Black people are mostly stupid. They drop out." They'll say stuff like, "So when are you dropping out?" like just assuming that 'cause I'm Black, I'm going to drop out of high school. As far as our Dress Code here, you know, I'm new here. I didn't know 'cause in the schools in L.A. you could dress totally different. So, I didn't know. One day, I had on some jeans. They had a little hole in them. But another girl came in wearing a skirt where you could see her butt. And the teacher didn't say anything. As soon as I walked in there, she was like "Dress Code violation!" So, I got sent to the office but they let me go back to class 'cause I told them that I didn't know. That same teacher has written me up plenty of times, yet girls in her class come in there revealing all kinds of stuff, even when it's cold.

At this school, honestly, there's not a lot of Black kids here. There's a lot of Hispanics and Caucasians. I'm not racist, but since I've been out here, I have been and I don't know why. Being out here has made me become racist as far as school and work. When I lived in L.A., I had four different jobs and out here it took me like six months to get a job. It's hard to find a job. I'll fill out the whole application and they would not call me. I was going to give up, but finally a Black supervisor at a store hired me and I'm thankful for that because I needed the money.

SUMMARY

This chapter yielded some good news and some bad news about racism in schools. Although the majority of the questionnaire respondents did not experience racism at their particular high school, 43 percent did. Moreover, a higher percentage of students who were in Special Education during elementary school said that they experienced racism at school. There was also a statistically significant correlation between grade retention in elementary school and experiencing racism during high school.

More than half of the students who experienced racism at school said that it occurred "occasionally" or "frequently." In most cases, the culprit was another student, but nearly one third of the students who experienced racism on campus said that an adult at school was the culprit. Most students did not report the racism to an adult on campus.

Even though the majority of the students did not experience racism themselves at school, nearly 60 percent said that they knew at least one other student who did. An even higher percentage of students said that although it is uncommon, racism does exist at their high school.

The good news is that most students did not think that they experienced overt racism themselves at school. The disturbing news, however, is that most students knew someone else who did, and most believed that racism, albeit uncommon, existed at their school. In fact, many students said that racial slurs are so common at school that they have learned to ignore them. Because students were the main culprits of racist behavior on campus, there appears to be a need for cultural awareness and cultural sensitivity issues to be addressed as part of the regular curriculum. There also appears to be a need for teachers and other adults on campus to receive cultural awareness and cultural sensitivity training, not only to deal with their own possible prejudicial mind-sets but also so that they can better equip students to get along across racial/ethnic lines.

Interestingly, students spoke about racial slurs, being singled out by teachers and other adults on campus, stereotypical comments being made, and physical altercations among racial/ethnic groups. They did not, however, discuss any of the institutional forms of racism. Comments throughout previous chapters clearly indicate that many students who participated in the study were victims of institutional racism in the forms of low expectations, a low level of instruction, poor counseling services, and grade inflation. Until these problems are rectified, the academic achievement of African American students will continue to lag behind that of their peers.

In conclusion, the results of the current study indicate that there is a need for racism in schools to be addressed both at the individual and the institutional levels. Some high school students and some adults on campus are subjecting students to racism. Students need to be taught how to get along with others of different racial/ethnic backgrounds. Adults on campus must be taught the same thing. Eradicating racism in schools starts with the proper mind-set and attitude about all members of the school community. Courage and a willingness to do whatever it takes to ensure that all members of the school community —regardless of race, socioeconomic status, and so on—feel welcome at the district office, in the school office, in the classroom, and at other locations on campus must follow. Hilliard (in Mabie, 2000) said that eliminating racism must begin with the acceptance that cultural diversity is a reality in American society. Unfortunately, "Diversity for some people is a very frightening concept" (p. 246).

For too long, leaders in most organizations—including schools—in American society have refused to take a stand about racism. They have not been courageous, and the majority have remained silent. Through their silence, they have given consent to racism. Because educators spend a considerable amount of time with children, the most vulnerable segment of American society, it is up to them to lead the way by undoing some of the damage, reversing negative trends, and eradicating longstanding policies and practices that have promoted institutional racism or permitted individualized racism to flourish in schools.

13

School Safety

According to the U.S. Departments of Education and Justice *Indicators of School Crime and Safety* (1999), teachers must have a safe learning environment to teach and students must have a safe environment in order to learn. Today, however, many students and teachers are concerned about being safe at school and are more likely than their predecessors to feel unsafe at school. Among students, elementary children are less likely than secondary students to be subjected to violence at school. Among teachers, middle school teachers are more likely than elementary or high school teachers to experience violence at school.

According to the U.S. Department of Education (2000), during the 1996–97 school year, nearly two thirds of all public schools reported a crime to police. The *Digest of Education Statistics (1999)* included data about the attitudes of teachers and students regarding numerous safety-related issues. The results of a "Schools and Staffing Survey" that was administered indicated that a higher percentage of public school teachers who were surveyed during the 1993 and 1994 school year versus those surveyed during the 1990 and 1991 school year considered physical conflicts among students at school, verbal abuse of teachers, student disrespect for teachers, and student possession of weapons to be serious problems.

Among students, perceptions regarding school safety vary according to gender and race or ethnicity. The *Digest of Education Statistics* (1999 & 2000) reported that during the 1997 and 1999 school years, higher percentages of African American and Hispanic high school students than Whites indicated that they felt too unsafe to go to school. In 1997, African American males were more likely than Hispanic or White males to report that they felt too unsafe to go to school, but Hispanic males were more likely than White males to do so. In 1999, however, Hispanic males were more than twice as likely as African American males to say that they felt too unsafe to attend school. In 1997, African American females were more likely than White females to state that they felt too unsafe to attend school, but Hispanic females were more likely than any group, male or female, to feel this way. Moreover, in 1999, Hispanic females were more likely than African American or White students to feel too unsafe to attend school, but African American females were more likely than Whites to do so. Furthermore, a higher percentage of African American females than African American males felt this way. Grade level also had some bearing on how students felt. During both years under review, a higher percentage of ninth graders than other high school students said that they felt unsafe, and ninth grade girls were more likely to do so than boys. Twelfth graders were least likely to say that they felt too unsafe to attend school.

When asked if they had carried a weapon to school, during both years, a higher percentage of ninth graders and eleventh graders said that they had. Additionally, at every grade level, a substantially higher percentage of males than females stated that they had done so. African American males were less likely than Hispanic or White males to say that they had carried a weapon on school property. African American females were more likely than White or Hispanic females to admit to it.

When asked if they had been in a physical fight on school property, ninth graders were more likely than other high school students to say that they had and seniors were least likely. Males were more likely than females to have been in a physical fight. African American and Hispanic males were more likely than White males to have been in a physical fight. Furthermore, a higher percentage of African American females than Whites and Hispanics reported that they had been in a fight at school.

The disproportionately high number of African American students, particularly African American males who are suspended or expelled from school, is one of the consequences of negative messages regarding fighting and aggression that individuals may internalize. Davis and Jordan (1995) said that a negative stigma is attached to suspension that could have long-term adverse consequences for African American students. This may also contribute to low self-esteem at school. Expulsion is even more serious than suspension.

In the county in which most of the 271 African American students who completed the survey for the current study resided, more than 1,500 students were expelled from school during the 1999–2000 school year. Fighting and threats of injury were the primary causes of expulsions, followed by drug- or alcohol-related problems and weapons on campus. Males accounted for 81 percent of the expulsions. Among secondary school students, a higher percentage of ninth graders, followed by eighth graders versus other secondary students, were expelled from school. In fact, eighth and ninth graders were almost four times as likely as seniors to be expelled from school. Although African American students comprised 11 percent of the total student population in the county, they comprised 18 percent of the expulsions. The students who participated in the interview phase of the current study were asked numerous questions relating to school safety, sexual harassment, suspension, and expulsion. The results are presented in this chapter.

SCHOOL SAFETY

The interviewees were asked whether or not they felt safe most of the time at their elementary, middle, and high schools. Most students said that they felt safe most of the time, but the percentage of students who felt unsafe increased with each level of schooling. For example, whereas only 7 percent said that they felt unsafe at their elementary school, 18 percent said that they felt unsafe at their middle school. Furthermore, 36 percent felt unsafe at their high school.

Explaining why she felt safe most of the time at her elementary school, one girl said, "I wasn't in a bad neighborhood. I never thought about crime. Nothing happened around there. Everybody knew each other. Everybody knew me, so I wasn't scared." One boy said that although he felt safe most of the time at his elementary school and high school, he felt unsafe at his middle school. "There were kids who did things that they shouldn't have done," he stated. "I saw knives, drugs, pepper spray, and I was actually stabbed once. A kid thought that I pushed his backpack onto the ground, which I didn't. He wanted me to pick it up and wash it all off, and all that. I told him that I didn't do it, and he stabbed me with a sharp metal piece of an umbrella." A girl who said that she felt safe most of the time at her elementary and middle school, said the converse was true of her high school. "I was late one day and the school was on lock down, because somebody on campus had guns," she said. "One time, I was walking home from school and this boy used to walk me to class all the time. I didn't even like him. His girlfriend came out of nowhere and she put a razor blade to my face."

Another girl said that she felt safe at her elementary and middle schools but felt so unsafe at her high school that she felt compelled to carry mace. She explained:

> I have a problem with girls. I got into a fight with them last year and then two fights during summer. Two girls tried to jump me when I was coming from summer school.

Every time I go out, I have to bring something. I take mace most of the time 'cause if there's a gang of girls, I'll just spray them in the face and just run. I had to do that here. At the other schools, I didn't have a problem 'cause I knew everyone. I think the girls out here are less secure 'cause I have always gotten along with everyone. I never got into any fights until I came out here.

I don't know. I have a lot of cute friends and a lot of ugly girls don't like my friends or something. We get mad and say "Ya'll just mad 'cause we cute." They were trying to jump me and my friends after school. They were in cars and we walk home from school. The school [officials] knows about it and they didn't do anything about it. It's like they were on their side. The girls that used to go here brought their older friends. One was 20. She went to jail for fighting a minor.

FEEDBACK ABOUT THE COLUMBINE TRAGEDY

The interviewees were also asked whether or not the tragedy that occurred at Columbine High School in Colorado could happen at the middle school or high school that they attended and what could be done to prevent similar situations from occurring. Half the interviewees said that they believed that a similar tragedy could occur at the middle school that they attended. Eighty-six percent said that they believed that it could happen at their high school.

The main reason that a high percentage of interviewees believed that similar situations could occur was that they felt that many students are ostracized or marginalized in schools. As a result, such students may retaliate through violence. One girl said, "The kids laugh at the kids who wear black clothes. They tell them that they are freaks and stuff." Another student said, "There are so many people that get teased and sit by themselves at lunch. That's a no no! You should not have anyone eating by themselves." A boy stated, "There are kids that get picked on here. About two percent are the kids that might make this kind of thing happen."

Another reason was that many students believed that "it could happen anywhere." A boy stated, "We got some crazy people that don't really care." Another boy said, "There are always students who don't get enough attention or something. It's not the teachers." A girl said, "There are just people out there that are going to do what they want to do, regardless, and I think that there's always a possibility that it could happen."

Several students said that they believed that White students in their school were more likely to create a Columbine-like situation. One girl said, "I'm not prejudiced but White people are crazy! You never know when a White kid will get mad at somebody or might pull a gun and shoot somebody 'cause they don't like him. I don't think no Black kid would do that." Another girl stated,

> There's a lot of off scale Caucasian kids here. The way they dress, all those piercings they have on their face, the way they talk. Yeah, I'm scared here. That could happen here. We've already had bomb threats. We had to evacuate one room in the school because of a bomb threat. Didn't nobody throw no bombs in L.A. Them kids couldn't even make no bomb if they tried!

The interviewees also had suggestions regarding what could be done to prevent similar situations from occurring. There were four recurring themes: (1) Prevention must begin before high school; (2) increase communication between adults and teenagers; (3) parents must teach their children to respect others; and (4) improve the school environment.

First, some interviewees felt that preventative measures should be taken long before high school. For example, one student said, "I think it's too late, because these kids got their own assumptions of what they want to do and they're going to do what they want to do. They don't respect the teachers. They should try to teach kids in junior high what respect is, to do what you have to do in school, and then do whatever you want to do out of school when you're not under the teacher's supervision." One girl said, "There's always a couple of people that think that everyone is against them, that no one cares about them. There's always a chance that something will go wrong and they're gonna take it out on everyone else."

Several students also felt that the best way to prevent future Columbine-like tragedies from happening is to increase the communication between adults and teenagers. One student advised adults to "talk to the students and know everything. Just find out what will make the school safer for everybody. Find out how the students feel about being in the classroom with the rest of the students or just being around campus." A girl said, "Teachers need to start listening and understanding kids and where they are coming from."

Several interviewees also said that parent involvement is crucial to preventing similar tragedies from occurring. One girl stated, "Parents need to get more involved with their kids." Another girl said, "I think if the parents instill positive things in the kids' head, then they won't think of bringing something like a gun to school." One girl advised parents to "let your kids be aware that they shouldn't tease anyone and make sure they include people that are not popular in their groups."

The fourth theme regarding how schools can prevent Columbine-like tragedies from occurring pointed to the need to improve the overall school environment. Some students wanted more metal detectors and a better way of screening visitors on campus. Another student felt that the quality of the security personnel should be upgraded. "All security guards need to get drug tested," she stated. "I've seen some of these security guards using drugs at work and I've seen them at some drug houses in the community."

Others wanted school officials to make more of an effort to make ostracized and marginalized students feel a sense of belonging. For example, one girl stated, "Teachers know that the jocks have an upper hand. They should not always praise the football player, because they make the people in sports feel better than any other regular person." Another girl said, "Teachers should have more control over their students and if they see any kind of problems going on, they should notify the principal or some kind of high authority." One boy advised schools to offer anger management classes. Another boy advised schools to offer clubs that promote self-esteem. One boy said simply, "You gotta make students like school." Another stated, "Just teach more teachers skills to recognize troubled students, have more programs at different schools, and pray." A girl who had been at a predominantly Black high school before transferring to her current school said that fostering a sense of community among the entire school population is crucial to preventing such tragedies from recurring. She explained:

> If the school came together as a family and everybody got along with everybody else, it wouldn't happen. At my old school, we used to have Pep Rallies and they were fun. Now, at this school, things are real dull and boring. At my old school, the principal used to walk around and talk to us. Here, the principal is this old White man that we don't even know. He doesn't even talk to us. At my old school, the teachers would come and talk to us and hang with us. Here the teachers don't do nothing.

SEXUAL HARASSMENT

The interviewees were also asked several questions about sexual harassment at their school. The majority said that they had never been sexually harassed at any level of their schooling, but 32 percent said that they had. All but one of the victims were girls, and most of the incidents occurred in high school versus elementary or middle school. Some students said that even though they were not sexually harassed themselves, they knew of others who were. At least one student blamed the victims. For example, one girl stated, "I've heard of it happening to other people, but I don't present myself in a way to be sexually harassed."

In all cases of sexual harassment, the culprit was another student. The types of sexual harassment ranged from suggestive or slanderous comments, to actual unwanted physical contact. The one boy who said that he was sexually harassed stated, "Starting in preschool, some girls were nasty. Some girl came and grabbed me and kissed me." From that point on, similar problems occurred in elementary school, middle school, and high school, he stated. A girl who said that she was sexually harassed at her high school stated, "Boys would make comments all the time, but I was raised to fight back." One girl said that five male students at her high school created a demeaning book about 75 girls at the school. The book was circulated around campus. She explained:

> Parents came down here and the guys got suspended, 'cause [school officials] didn't want to see any Black guys go to jail. They had a book and it talked about all body parts, everything you could think of. They were giving it to guys around the school and the guys would come up to us and ask if they could do certain things with us. I told them, "I'm not even that type of person" and they said "So and so wrote a book. Look. See, your name is in here."
>
> The parents came and they had police up here. Mr. [a school official] said, "Well, I don't want to see too many Black guys going to jail." I think they got suspended for two days because I just saw one of them here today.
>
> The boy who started the book was a White boy. I guess the girls started a book about them, and then the guys started a book about the girls. That's supposedly what they said. But we haven't seen a book around here that girls made against the guys. We saw the book about the girls that the guys made. It was just too much. This White boy talks about Black girls and White girls. He says that White girls are pretty but he talks about the Black girls bad.

Unlike the girl who was involved in the aforementioned incident, most of the students who said that they were sexually harassed did not report it to any school official. A girl who said that an older male student routinely made sexually suggestive comments to her and then began to pressure her to become intimate with him explained, "When it occurred, I didn't really look at it as sexual harassment, but now that I'm older, I can see. I was upset about the whole situation, but you don't think about it. Now, I look at it and I think 'Man, he could have really gotten in trouble for that.'" Another student said that she didn't report the sexual harassment that she was subjected to during high school because "Guys say things all the time. Even if you report it, they'll just go to somebody else."

Conversely, most interviewees said that they had never sexually harassed another student but a few interviewees, all males, said "no comment." One male, however, admitted that he had sexually harassed another student during middle school. Another boy stated, "I was always too afraid. I was afraid the girls would beat me up."

SUSPENSION AND EXPULSION

Thirty-six percent of the interviewees said that they had been suspended from school at least once, and several had been suspended multiple times. In the majority of cases, the cause was fighting, but most students said that they only fought in self-defense. Some students were also suspended for having conflicts with teachers. One student said that he was suspended for having too many tardies.

Fifty percent of the suspensions occurred during the middle school years as opposed to 31 percent during the high school years and only 18 percent during the elementary years. The period during which the suspensions occurred, began during fourth grade and ended in eleventh grade. For some reason, there were no suspensions during tenth grade or twelfth grade. Moreover, there were no suspensions prior to fourth grade.

Only 2 percent of the interviewees said that they had been expelled from school, and in each case, they disagreed with how school officials handled the situation.

One girl said that she was expelled for wearing an earring on her finger that was perceived to be a deadly weapon. "No one even listened to me," she complained. "They went through everything. They read my journal and they highlighted things. I was taken to jail. I was out of school for a whole month and half until a Due Process Hearing was held. Then, they put me on a contract." Another girl was expelled during elementary school for hitting a teacher who was hurting her arm. She felt that she was treated unfairly by school officials because "all the kids were trying to tell the principal what happened and they weren't listening to us. They were like, 'This is an adult and you shouldn't hit an adult.'" A boy who was kept out of school for two months for fighting during sixth grade stated, "They really tried to kick me out but I moved to a different school."

SUMMARY

This chapter explored issues related to school safety. The majority of the interviewees said that they felt safe most of the time at school, but the percentage who felt unsafe increased with each level of schooling. Conflicts with peers surfaced in several narratives in previous chapters. Both male and female students might benefit from conflict-resolution strategies. Because conflicts appear to increase as students age, elementary school might be the best period to begin such training. The training should stress the importance of treating oneself and others, both adults and students, respectfully. Thereafter, ongoing training during each school year might be beneficial. Since ninth grade is known to be a crucial period when students are more apt to feel too unsafe to attend school (*Digest of Education Statistics*, 1999 & 2000), it is imperative that such training be provided well before ninth grade but also that additional services be offered to ninth graders. As noted previously, the students who participated in the current study resided in a region that not only had a low college attendance rate, but it also had a high ninth grade dropout rate. Issues relating to school safety might contribute to students dropping out of school.

Although the majority of the interviewees said that they felt safe at school, the majority also believed that a tragedy similar to the Columbine shooting incident could occur at their high school. Furthermore, half of the interviewees believed that such a tragedy could have occurred at their previous middle school. Students were concerned that many students feel marginalized in school and that these individuals might erupt in violence. They said that teasing and loneliness are two of the underlying reasons some students act out violently in school. Although a few of the school shootings nationwide have been initiated by Black students, some students in the current study seemed unaware of this fact. Therefore, they assumed that Whites are the only students who are capable of such behavior. When schools become more proactive regarding safety issues, conflict-resolution training, and increasing communication between adults on campus and students, such naiveté is likely to disappear.

Although the majority of the interviewees were not sexually harassed at school, the fact that one third of the students, mostly girls, were cannot be ignored. All students, as noted at the beginning of this chapter, must feel safe in order to learn. When students fear sexual harassment or any type of harassment or unsafe condition at school, their ability to perform at optimum levels will undoubtedly decrease. Urban students are particularly likely to have to perform under stressful conditions (Haberman, 1995). As many of the interviewees stressed, there is a great need to improve the overall climate and environment of many schools. The starting point, as students recommended, is fostering a sense of community not only on a schoolwide level but also on a classroom level. Schools and classrooms must become more inclusive and less exclusive. Principals and other administrators must set the appropriate tone by modeling positive behavior. They should be visible on campus, and they should attempt to get to know as many students on a personal and first-name basis as possible. Teachers should follow suit (Haberman, 1995).

Whereas only 2 percent of the interviewees had been expelled from school, nearly 40 percent had been suspended at least once from school. Davis and Jordan (1995) noted that suspensions had an adverse effect on high school grades. Moreover, multiple suspensions had an even more detrimental effect on grades. Several narratives and additional comments from students indicate that African American students appear to be sent out of class or given Referrals routinely. Although this issue was not addressed in the study, it has surfaced as a problem that must be examined if achievement scores of African American students are expected to improve.

Payne (1998), for example, attributed the high rate of discipline problems of students from impoverished backgrounds to ignorance. Teachers are ignorant of the reasons students behave as they do, not realizing that certain behaviors that are disparaged at school are crucial to survival in the students' home environment. On the other hand, because schools are based on middle-class norms, students from impoverished backgrounds are often doomed to failure because they have not been taught the skills that are necessary for survival in schools. Instead of assuming that inappropriate classroom behavior should always warrant a Referral, suspension, or expulsion, Payne urged educators to provide students with alternatives in the form of acceptable behaviors. In the case of the use of inappropriate language from students, for example, she suggested that teachers offer students "other phrases that could be used to say the same thing" (p. 103). When students laugh when they are disciplined, teachers might tell them explicitly why laughter is inappropriate in this instance. When students resort to physical fighting at school, teachers should help them to develop a list of acceptable options. To prevent excessive talking in class, teachers should develop lessons that involve more class participation.

One of the successful teachers of African American children that Ladson-Billings (1994) described was aware that African American "students are always being blamed for things they don't know" (p. 65). Because African American children were being blamed for misbehaving in the school cafeteria, this teacher modeled proper table manners, healthy eating, and how to plan meals for her students by inviting them to help prepare and eat meals at her own home on a regular basis. Another successful teacher of African American students would invite small groups of students to lunch each week. Instead of holding these African American children accountable for "hidden rules" that they had not been taught, these teachers chose to actually teach them the rules.

The bottom line is that African American students who come from lower socioeconomic backgrounds must be equipped with the tools that are necessary for success in schools. These tools not only include the strong reading, writing, and math foundation that are pivotal to academic success but also the inter- and intrapersonal skills that are obligatory for survival in schools. When teachers take the time to (a) learn why African American children behave as they do and (b) explicitly teach African American students, starting in elementary school, the rules of the culture of power (Delpit, 1995), fewer African American students will be singled out for discipline and punishment, which often is the precursor to the downward spiral of poor achievement.

14

Parent Involvement

In *Predictors of Resilience in African American Adults*, Thompson (1998) examined a number of topics that pertained to African Americans who are considered to be successful by traditional standards and also African American college students. One of the findings was that most of the participants in the study said that they had positive role models during childhood and/or adolescence. Parents were the most commonly cited group of role models, followed by another relative, and then, thirdly, teachers.

In her five-month study of 20 African American high school seniors from poor families, Floyd (1995) found several factors that contributed to the students' academic success. One of her major findings was that these students had experienced good parental relationships or positive relationships with some other significant adult, such as grandparents, church members, or school employees. Most of these students had parents who were very active in their children's lives. They were involved in school activities, knew their children's friends, and were aware of their whereabouts as often as possible.

Hurd, Moore, and Rogers (1995) found that most of the African American parents in their study were extremely involved in their children's lives. These parents emphasized effort and achievement, respect for others, and self-reliance. Hurd et al. selected 53 participants in North Carolina and interviewed them over a three-month period. The researchers found that the parents tried to teach their children to view life as a "testing ground," to have pride in their culture, and to cultivate a spiritual relationship with God. The subjects also reported that they relied heavily on extended family members, which is a common theme in the literature about African American families. The results of the aforementioned studies illustrate how highly esteemed parents were in the eyes of the study participants. Conversely, there is a widespread belief in educational circles that Black parents do not really care about their children's education.

In its "Schools and Staffing Survey" for 1990–91 and 1993–94, the *Digest of Education Statistics* reported that out of all the issues that public school teachers considered to be serious problems at their school, lack of parental involvement was one of the most frequently cited. In another study, "Teachers' Perceptions About Teaching and School Conditions," the *Digest of Education Statistics* (1999) revealed that slightly more than half the public school teachers surveyed believed that they received a great deal of support from parents for the work that they did. A higher percentage of elementary than secondary teachers believed this. Conversely, more than 80 percent of the private school teachers believed this.

Numerous researchers have offered reasons why some parents refuse to become visibly involved in their children's education. Comer and Poussaint (1992) stressed the important role that Black parents can play in their children's academic achievement. In describing the variety of attitudes regarding education that are prevalent in the Black community, they noted that although most Black parents view education as a means to a positive end, an "anti-intellectual" attitude does exist among some members of the community. One reason is that some Black parents have ambivalent feelings regarding transmitting the values of White society to their children. In "The Silenced Dialogue," Delpit (1995) described ways in which educators unwittingly silence the "voices" of parents and students of color. One theory is that many parents retain memories of negative schooling experiences from their own childhoods (Cunningham & Allington, 1999; Fields & Spangler, 2000). Another theory is that parents may perceive the school to be an unwelcoming environment (Fields & Spangler, 2000; Poplin & Weeres, 1992; Smith, 1986). Smith (1986) noted that teachers focus more on negatives than positives when contacting parents regarding their children. Comer and Poussaint (1992) and Fields and Spangler (2000) found that some parents feel uncomfortable around teachers because of their own limited education.

One clear message from research is that misunderstandings are common between educators and parents (Delpit, 1995; Harris & Sipay, 1990). On the one hand, parents may feel that they are not wanted at school (Delpit, 1995; Smith, 1986). Conversely, educators often perceive parents' absence from school events and minimal contact with teachers as a lack of interest in their children's academic welfare (Delpit, 1995; Haberman, 1995).

A number of researchers have found, however, that most parents, including those of children from nonmainstream backgrounds value education and are extremely concerned about how their children are faring in schools (Gunning, 2000). Flores, Teff-Cousins, and Diaz (1991) debunked the myth that Hispanic parents are unconcerned about their children's education. Darder (1991) said that many parents of color make huge sacrifices to ensure that their children get educated.

Poplin and Weeres (1992) also refuted the myth that the parents of children of color do not care about their children's academic progress. Indeed, they found that parents want more dialogue with teachers. Furthermore, many parents are concerned that negative relationships between their children and teachers are damaging to their children. Poplin and Weeres concluded that although it may appear that certain parents do not have strong education-related values for their children, they merely express these values in culturally different ways than some mainstream teachers understand.

Today, it is clear to educators and policymakers that education must involve all sectors of the community, including parents, particularly when it comes to improving the reading and writing skills of children (Au, 1993; Gunning, 2000, Harris & Sipay, 1990; Routman, 1996, Ruddell, 1999; Smith, 1986). Moreover, experts have acknowledged the power of parents to impede or derail educational policies and instructional practices. Routman (1996) stressed that educational change will be ineffective without parental involvement at every level of the change process. More importantly, literacy begins at home, not at school. Therefore, parents play an invaluable role in literacy acquisition (Harris & Sipay, 1990). Harris and Sipay said that when parents of struggling readers are unaware of proper methods to use to assist their children, they can actually exacerbate children's reading problems.

The 271 African American students who participated in the current study were asked to rate the quality of their parents' or guardians' involvement in their elementary, middle school, and high school education, particularly regarding homework, meeting with teachers, and attending school functions. The results are presented in this chapter.

PARENTAL INVOLVEMENT DURING
ELEMENTARY SCHOOL

The majority of students rated their parents' involvement in their education during elementary school as "excellent" or "good," and only 7 percent rated it as "poor." A higher percentage of students who were in Special Education during elementary school rated it as "fair." A higher percentage of students who were in G.A.T.E. during elementary school rated it as "excellent" (see Table 14-1). There was a statistically significant correlation between how students rated the quality of their parents' involvement in their elementary education and how they rated the overall quality of instruction provided by their elementary school teachers ($r = .25; p < .001$).

One girl said, "In fourth grade, I had a lot of family problems, so I kind of fell off with my school work. But my parents have always been supportive. When that role was taken away for a short period of time, it affected me. I think it got me down, but then it helped me to want to succeed even more."

PARENTAL INVOLVEMENT DURING MIDDLE SCHOOL

Most students gave a high rating to their parents' or guardians' involvement in their middle school education. With the exception of elementary Special Education students, which remained the same, the percentage of students who rated it as "fair" or "poor" was higher for the middle school years than for the elementary years. Consequently, the percentage who rated it as "good" or "excellent" during the middle school years was also lower for most groups.

A higher percentage of students who were in Special Education during elementary school rated their parents' or guardians' middle school versus elementary school involvement as "excellent." There was only a slight difference, however, between the percentage who rated it as "good" or "excellent" when the two were combined. Conversely, there were larger differences between how students who were retained or in basic or G.A.T.E. elementary classes rated their parents' or guardians' involvement in their middle school education. For both groups, the percentage that rated it as "good" or "excellent" for middle school was lower. For elementary G.A.T.E. students, it was almost 20 percentage points lower (see Table 14-2).

TABLE 14-1
How Students Rated Their Parents'/Guardians' Involvement in Their Elementary School Education (by % of Students and Their Elementary Group)

Rating	Total Sample	Retainees	SpecEd.	Basic	G.A.T.E.
Poor	7	12	0	7	5
Fair	19	15	36	20	16
Good	35	42	55	35	32
Excellent	39	31	9	37	46

N = 271

TABLE 14-2
How Students Rated Their Parents'/Guardians' Involvement in Their Middle School Education (by % of Students and Elementary Group)

Rating	Total Sample	Retainees	SpecEd.	Basic	G.A.T.E.
Poor	9	19	9	9	11
Fair	27	23	27	28	23
Good	30	27	27	31	29
Excellent	32	27	36	32	30

N = 271

PARENTAL INVOLVEMENT DURING HIGH SCHOOL

The majority of students also rated the overall quality of their parents' or guardians' involvement in their high school education as "good" or "excellent." However, the percentage of students in the total sample who rated it as "poor" increased, and the percentage who rated it as "good" or "excellent" decreased.

One of the most obvious changes in students' previous ratings was that those who were in Special Education during elementary school appeared to be a lot more satisfied with the level of their parents' or guardians' involvement in their high school education than with parental involvement during elementary or middle school. Students who were in G.A.T.E. during elementary school were less likely than any of the three groups to assign a high rating to their parents' or guardians' involvement in their high school education (see Table 14-3).

SUMMARY

Most students gave a high rating to their parents' involvement at every level of their schooling. With each level of their schooling, however, student satisfaction decreased, but overall it remained high. Un-

TABLE 14-3
How Students Rated Their Parents'/Guardians' Involvement in Their High School Education (by % of Students and Their Elementary Group)

Rating	Total Sample	Retainees	SpecEd.	Basic	G.A.T.E.
Poor	13	12	9	12	18
Fair	28	27	9	28	29
Good	29	23	46	29	29
Excellent	30	38	36	31	23

N = 271

like most other students, those who were in elementary Special Education classes appeared to be more satisfied with their parents' involvement during high school versus elementary or middle school. Many students who were in G.A.T.E. during elementary school appeared to be particularly displeased with their parents' involvement in their secondary level schooling.

Herein lies a conundrum. Public school educators routinely blame the poor academic achievement of African American students on a lack of parental involvement. Teachers complain that parents are uninterested in their children's education (Delpit, 1995). They assume that poorly attended school events and a lack of parent-initiated contact are signs that African American parents do not care about their children's academic success or failure. As a result, it becomes convenient for teachers to excuse their own low expectations and ineffective teaching practices by blaming the students for being apathetic and by blaming their parents for not caring.

The results of the current chapter reveal, however, that most African American students in this study gave a high rating to their parents' or guardians' involvement at all three levels of their schooling. Moreover, several narratives and students' comments that were presented in previous chapters show why this is so. For example, in chapter 9, Tisha's narrative stressed that her parents placed such a strong value on education that they made her school work and homework a priority, even when she was ill. They also were so dissatisfied with the low standards and lack of rigor at Tisha's elementary school, that they transferred her to another school that had higher standards. In chapter 2, more than half the interviewees said that during elementary school, their mothers read to them regularly, and one fourth said that their fathers did. Celeste, the student who did not learn to read until high school, said that she relied heavily on her mother's assistance to survive elementary school. Marcel's parents encouraged him to read, they read to him regularly, and his father motivated him to read "Black" books that had a high readability level.

Other students shared how their parents or guardians provided other means of support for their schooling that were invisible to teachers. For example, students who experienced racism at school were more likely to report it to a parent or guardian and least likely to report it to an adult at school. Several students stated that when they were singled out or harassed by teachers, their parents shared coping strategies with them (McAdoo, 1992). Some parents helped their children by discussing their own experiences with discrimination with them.

One of the strongest ways that the parents or guardians of the African American students in this study showed how much they valued education was by encouraging their children to attend college. The majority of the interviewees said that at least one family member or relative had urged them to go to college. In fact, several students said that one reason why they planned to attend college was to make their family proud. One student said that going to college would enable her to assist her family financially. In chapter 7, JaVon stated that his family had not only encouraged him to go to college, but his parents had started stressing this during his elementary school years.

The high ratings that most of the African American students gave to their parents' or guardians' involvement in their schooling is also noteworthy for another reason. As noted previously, most of the students who participated in the study lived in an area that had a high child poverty rate, low college attendance rate, and high ninth grade dropout rate. Several narratives pointed out that some of the students and their families had experienced hardships relating to financial problems, divorce, chronic moving from one location to another, substance abuse, and even physical abuse. Therefore, it is likely that many of the students' parents lived under highly stressful conditions. Nevertheless, the majority of parents or guardians—at least by their children's standards—were highly involved in their children's schooling.

It is clear that a dichotomy exists between what educators have traditionally stated about Black parents' involvement in their children's schooling and what the African American students in the current study said about their parents' or guardians' involvement. One explanation might be that educators are using a limited paradigm to measure parent involvement. Apparently, many African American parents are attempting to assist their children in ways that are not always obvious to educators. For example, Ladson-Billings (1994) described how her own parents rarely went to her school, but they provided strong support for her education by expecting her to get good grades and to behave in school.

There is an obvious need for more dialogue between parents and educators to alleviate misunderstandings and ignorance. The importance of the parental impact and connecting with the community in which students reside has been stressed by researchers. Moreover, there was a statistically significant correlation between how students rated their parents' or guardians' involvement in their elementary school education and how they rated the overall quality of instruction provided by most of their elementary teachers. It appears, therefore, that parent involvement during elementary school is linked to the quality of instruction that African American students receive. Forty-one percent of the students who completed the questionnaire also recommended that in order to better prepare students for college, educators must find ways to increase parental involvement. Many students said that their "best" teachers initiated contact with their parents.

Because many African American parents "feel uncomfortable and intimidated with professional people" (Comer and Poussaint, 1992, p. 190), they may be unlikely to attend school functions and initiate contact with teachers. Nevertheless, the results of the current chapter emphasize the fact that African American parents are concerned about their children's schooling and are making attempts to assist them. White and Parham (1990) urged educators to assist African American parents by providing them with feedback about how to help their children excel academically. A strong partnership between African American parents and teachers can undoubtedly improve the academic achievement of African American children. The creation of a monthly, student-centered class newsletter, describing special events pertaining to each classroom—upcoming assignments, project due dates, and suggestions on how parents can assist their children is one option. This newsletter can be written and designed by students. In addition to providing their parents with useful information, it can also improve students' writing skills and give them an authentic way to utilize their writing skills. Parents might be more likely to read a newsletter consisting of articles and artwork that are created by their children. Another option is to use parents as a resource. At the beginning of the school year, teachers might send a brief questionnaire to parents or ask students to interview their parents. The goal is to find out what unique background experiences parents have had that they might be able to share with the class. For example, a parent who served in the Gulf War might be invited to give a history lesson from a personal perspective. Parents who have traveled abroad or who work in law enforcement, health care, or the entertainment industry might also be invited to give presentations. Parents might also be invited to do brief presentations on historical figures who made an impact on them. The key is to find multiple opportunities to invite parents into classrooms and to convince them that they are truly welcome in schools.

In the case of parents who are unable to assist their children academically because of their own weak skills, schools can provide an on-site parent center. This center can offer tutorial services for parents to improve their own skills. Because many parents have poor parenting skills as a result of their own upbringing or the fact that they were teenage mothers, the on-site parent center might also offer ongoing parenting workshops. Delpit (1995) stressed, however, that effective parent workshops must be built on the realities with which African American parents live. Thus, workshop facilitators must have ample background knowledge of the sociocultural context of the parents' communities.

There are many other options that educators should explore if they are sincerely committed to increasing the involvement of African American parents. One important point to remember, however, is that good teachers do not waste time assigning blame to parents or to students. They are too busy working on improving the quality of instruction that they offer. Although they make attempts to telephone parents and to contact them by mail, they do not give up on children merely because the parents are not behaving as the teachers deem fit. They accept the fact that some things are out of their control and they move forward in spite of this. In describing their "best" teachers, many of the African American students in this study said that these teachers treated them "like family" and formed personal relationships with them. Hilliard (in Mabie, 2000) surmised that "what is essential in school is the relationships. The engine that really drives good instruction is the bond between a teacher and a student" (p. 250). Ladson-Billings (1994) repeatedly stressed that the successful teachers of African American children that she studied cultivated relationships with students that went beyond the classroom and they were connected to each of their students. These teachers invited students to their homes and invited them to participate in activities away from school.

In summary, parental involvement is important, and teachers should make every effort to increase it. They should not, however, use parents as an excuse to shirk their own responsibilities. Moreover, they should not underestimate their power to make a positive impact on students regardless of the level of parental involvement.

15

Conclusion

Nearly four decades ago, Clark (1965) described the plight of African American students. Because of their inferior status in schools, as well as disparagement and disrespect from educators, Clark argued that the students developed contempt for their teachers and the educational system. With that in mind, the feedback from the African American students who participated in the current study shows that some progress has been made for African American students, yet there is still much work to be done.

Students made many positive comments about their teachers. Many felt that most of their teachers had done a good job and many described their "best" teachers in glowing terms. The recurring themes that surfaced from this study can provide educators and policymakers with invaluable information that can be useful in closing the achievement gap between African American students and their peers of other races/ethnicities.

Although most of the students in the current study did not express contempt for their teachers or for the educational system, "disappointment" was definitely a recurring theme. African American students clearly want more from the educational system, their teachers, and the curriculum than they are getting. The strongest messages from the students involve the effects of tracking, ineffective instructional practices, relationships with teachers and peers, problems with the curriculum, and preparing African American students for college. What became most noticeable is that schools actually contribute to African American underachievement through a number of common but destructive practices. Despite the fact that the majority of students tended to give a high rating to the overall quality of instruction provided by most of their elementary and secondary school teachers, the "educational default" and "ineffective teaching methods" that Clark (1965) criticized and "the lack of sustained effort to provide quality education for African Americans" that Ladson-Billings (1994, p. 4) described became evident in a number of ways.

Starting in elementary school, many students were subjected to practices that actually "turned them off" to reading. Even though most of the African American students who participated in the interview phase of the study said that they had been good readers during elementary school, many said that they did not find reading enjoyable. The students desired a wider selection of books that would interest them. Many felt that the books that they were offered were boring and outdated. In addition to the limited selection of books in the classroom and school libraries, some students got the impression that the school library was off limits to African American students.

Others said that they were unaware that the library even existed, or because of the limited book selection, they only used it for school-related purposes instead of for recreational reading. The fact that Celeste, whose narrative was shared in chapter 2, made it all the way to tenth grade without being able to read is alarming. Not only were most of her elementary and middle school teachers unable to detect the cause of her reading difficulty, but they also did not know how to assist her. After studying five different reading methods, Hilliard (in Mabie, 2000) found that all of them were effective, not because of the method but because of good teaching practices. As Thompson (2000) concluded, there is a great need for elementary and secondary teachers to receive more training regarding the teaching of reading. Given that NAEP (National Center for Education Statistics, 1999) has repeatedly reported that the average African American fourth, eighth, and twelfth grader has weaker reading skills than his/her counterparts of other racial/ethnic groups, this would, undoubtedly, have a positive effect on African American students' achievement.

Second, evidence of problems with the math curriculum and instructional practices starting in middle school and proliferating in high school appeared numerous times throughout the study. The majority of students who participated in the study failed at least one high school course, and math was the subject that they were most likely to have failed. Math was also cited as the "most difficult" middle school and high school subject for most students. Moreover, math teachers were more likely than others to be identified as "worst" middle school and high school teachers. Indeed, the "educational neglect," particularly when it comes to mathematics instruction, for African American students, that Polite (1999) described became evident.

Additionally, evidence of grade inflation, low expectations, and a low level of instruction surfaced throughout the study. Students described the curriculum as "boring, irrelevant, and nonchallenging." They referred to assignments as "baby work" and "busy work." They talked about being required to do assignments as punishment for being noisy in class and then were told that they did not have to even hand the work in. Students also said that in some classes all they had to do was show up to receive a passing grade. Several students also sensed that certain teachers expected them to fail.

The detrimental effects of tracking and labeling students during elementary school were also apparent. Undoubtedly, the study disclosed that African American public school students within the same school, the same school district, or within the same city can receive a markedly different caliber of instruction. Although the African American students in the current study were not overrepresented in the Special Education program, starting in elementary school, students who were retained or placed in the Special Education program had noticeably different schooling experiences. For the most part, they tended to report more negative experiences. Alexander, Entwisle, and Dauber's (1994) assertion that even when students are retained they tend to remain behind academically for the duration of their years in school appears to be validated by this study.

Likewise, even students who were in basic and college preparatory classes complained about low teacher expectations, a low level of instruction, and alluded to grade inflation. Conversely, students who were placed in G.A.T.E. during elementary school appeared to be chosen for success. In most cases, their schooling experiences tended to be more positive than those of others. Nevertheless, some G.A.T.E. students had negative schooling experiences. Furthermore, the percentage of students who were in G.A.T.E. during elementary school had dwindled to nearly half its size by the time students reached high school. The loneliness and isolation that prompted Briana, whose narrative was included in chapter 1, to voluntarily leave the G.A.T.E. program also might have contributed to the lower percentage of students who were in G.A.T.E. during high school. Therefore, being chosen for the G.A.T.E. program appears to benefit African American students in that they receive a better quality of instruction and they tend to express more satisfaction with their homework and the overall quality of instruction that they receive. However, it is problematic because the low number of African American students who are in G.A.T.E., Advanced Placement, and Honors classes at the high school level causes students to experience culture shock. Although the sample sizes for elementary retainees and Special Education students were too small for definitive conclusions to be drawn, analyses of questionnaire results and students' comments indicate that wide disparities exist in students' schooling experiences according to their academic tracks (Hacker, 1992; Oakes, 1999). Thus, tracking, starting in elementary school, not only contributes to low achievement among African American students but it also appears to have a strong effect on subsequent schooling experiences.

Not only had the majority of the interviewees planned to attend college, but most had already applied to colleges and universities at the time of their interview. Yet many expressed disappointment in the quality of preparation that they received for college and also the quality of services that they received from their high school counselors. Students complained of not being told how to apply for college or when the deadlines were. Some mentioned that counselors attempted to dissuade them from applying to four-year universities. As in Polite's (1999) study, the students expected more from their counselors than they actually received.

The students' recommendations regarding how schools can better prepare students for college are enlightening. African American students want teachers to teach them better study skills and they want teachers and counselors to provide them with more information about college. They want more students to have access to college preparatory classes, and they want better math preparation. Many also indicated that better teachers must be hired.

The most prevalent and overarching theme emanating from the current study is that more than anything else "good teaching matters" (Haycock, 1998), and it is possibly the key determinant of African American student achievement (Clark, 1965; Collins, 1992; Hare & Hare, 1991; Hilliard, in Mabie, 2000; Kunjufu, 1990, 1985; Ladson-Billings, 1994; Polite, 1999; White & Parham, 1990). For African American students, good teachers use certain instructional practices and possess the characteristics that African American students deem important. For example, according to the African American students in the current study, good teachers (a) make the course work and subject matter comprehensible by explaining things well; (b) they make the course work interesting; (c) instead of discouraging African American students from asking questions, they are patient and they give extra help; (d) instead of singling out African American students unnecessarily for punishment and discipline, they are fair; (e) instead of exhibiting coolness, fear, and aloofness toward their African American students, they are friendly; (f) instead of using a boring instructional delivery that will create discipline problems, apathy, and disinterest, they use humor in their method of delivery; (g) and instead of offering African American students a watered down curriculum that is based on low expectations, they challenge students academically.

More than anything, however, successful teachers of African American students must possess a certain mind-set. Instead of expecting deficits, teachers must look for the innate talents and gifts that all African American students arrive at school with. They must be willing to first see their African American students as human beings who have a rich history and a strong culture that should be incorporated into the curriculum. They must realize that their African American students want equitable and fair relationships with them that extend beyond the classroom (Ladson-Billings, 1994). These relationships must be built on trust, mutual respect, and a sincere desire to provide African American students with the best caliber of instruction that teachers can offer.

Unfortunately, one of the strongest messages emerging from this study is that many educators "cop out" by assuming that it is impossible for them to reach African American students. Deficit theorists have promoted the notion that some students, particularly those from problematic and minority backgrounds, can be ignored because there is no hope for them. In other words, their problems or "deficits" are insurmountable. Because of this widespread viewpoint among some educators, teachers can justify or excuse the low quality of instruction that they offer to these students. Many of the comments from the African American students indicated that this was indeed the case for them. Several said that teachers were "only there for a paycheck."

The current study shows, however, that regardless of the background from which students come, outstanding teachers can make a powerful impact on the lives of their African American students (Ladson-Billings, 1994; Thompson, 1998). Many students who were interviewed for this study experienced stressful and even traumatic circumstances during childhood and/or adolescence. Child abuse, drug addiction, poverty, the death of a parent, divorce or separation, being harassed at school, and moving frequently and having to make new friends and adjust to a new environment were some of the problems that students described. Given the research on the causes and effects of Post Traumatic Stress Disorder (PTSD), it is even possible that some of the interviewees may have suffered from PTSD (Garbarino et al., 1992). In spite of the challenging circumstances during childhood and/or adolescence that many students experienced, they persevered. They not only remained in school all the way through their senior year, but most of the interviewees planned to attend college as well. The students' resiliency and determination to become successful adults radiated throughout the narratives. They were not hopeless; they were hopeful. Many realized that they had been inadequately prepared for college, yet they had high hopes of succeeding. The following lists, which combine feedback from the students and researchers who have studied African American students, summarize some key points that educators should remember in their efforts to close the achievement gap for African American students.

CLOSING THE ACHIEVEMENT GAP: RECOMMENDATIONS FOR EDUCATIONAL POLICYMAKERS AND SCHOOL ADMINISTRATORS

1. Acknowledge that institutional racism is embedded in the educational system.
2. Conduct a needs assessment to identify the ways in which institutional racism continues to have an adverse effect on the achievement of African American students. Be sure to include African American parents, educators, and community leaders in the dialogue.
3. Prioritize the aspects of institutional racism, such as tracking, low teacher expectations, underprepared teachers, a lack of instructional rigor, and the like that must be addressed first.
4. Develop an action plan that includes anticipated outcomes, timelines, and the like.
5. Implement the action plan.
6. Hold people accountable.
7. Require ongoing cultural awareness and diversity workshops for district personnel, administrators, teachers, school support staff, and students.
8. Require all district and school office personnel to take ongoing customer service training and hold individuals responsible for rude and unprofessional behavior toward parents and students.
9. Tour schools and classrooms on a regular basis.
10. Require district officials and school administrators to "sub" in classrooms on a regular basis so that they can stay in touch with the realities of the classroom.
11. Reduce the top-heavy district office staff and return the surplus staff to the local school sites. This would reduce class size.
12. Hire social workers or counselors who can provide true counseling to students.
13. Improve the quality of services that school counselors provide about college.
14. Find funding for more field trips to colleges and invite guest speakers to discuss the college experience with students.
15. Provide SAT/ACT preparation courses to all high school students, starting in ninth grade.
16. Adopt a "zero tolerance" policy regarding racist practices.

17. Hire teachers who believe that all children can learn, regardless of race or socioeconomic status.

RECOMMENDATIONS FOR TEACHER TRAINING PROGRAMS

1. Use multiple methods of determining who is qualified to teach.
2. Increase efforts to recruit African American teachers, by creating a mentoring program for secondary students of color who might be interested in becoming teachers.
3. Increase the number of cultural awareness and diversity courses that pre-service and practicing teachers are required to take.
4. Stress the correlations between student achievement and teacher expectations and attitudes toward students.
5. Do not assign a passing grade to student teachers who demonstrate biased or racist behavior when you observe them teach.

RECOMMENDATIONS FOR TEACHERS

1. Get to know your students on a personal basis and strive to form positive relationships with them.
2. Have high expectations for all students.
3. Make the curriculum relevant to students' lives outside the classroom.
4. Use clear and comprehensible communication.
5. Teach students the "hidden rules" of mainstream society.
6. Create a collaborative versus competitive classroom.
7. Uncover students' gifts and talents.
8. Educate yourself about African American culture and use this knowledge as you design lesson plans.
9. Be willing to offer extra assistance to students.
10. Upgrade your skills and knowledge base on a regular basis by attending conferences and workshops and reading educational journals and books.
11. Make the course work interesting by inviting students to assist you and make suggestions as you design lessons.
12. Give students lots of opportunities to do hands-on activities and projects.
13. Use multicultural texts in your curriculum and stock your classroom library with a diverse selection of books.
14. Assign meaningful and an appropriate amount of homework.
15. Find ways to convince African American parents that you value their input and that they are welcome in your classroom.

16. Review regularly the list of "Qualities of Outstanding Educators" (see chapter 3) that African American students deem important and use it as a checklist to determine the areas of your teaching that you need to improve.
17. Strengthen your own reading, writing, and math skills.

References

Alexander, K. L., Entwisle, D. R. & Dauber, S. L. (1994). *On the success of failure: A reassessment of the effects of retention in the primary grades*. New York: Cambridge University Press.

Au, K. H. (1993). *Literacy instruction in multicultural settings*. Austin, TX: Holt, Rinehart and Winston, Inc.

Barr, R. D., & Parrett, W. H. (1995). *Hope at last for at-risk youths*. Needham Heights, MA: Allyn & Bacon.

Burdman, P. (2000). Extra credit, extra criticism. *Black Issues in Higher Education*, 17(18), 28–33.

California Department of Education. (2000). Sacramento.

Chall, J. S. (1967). *Learning to read: The great debate*. New York: McGraw-Hill Book Company.

Chideya, F. (1995). *Don't believe the hype*. New York: Penguin Books.

Clark, K. B. (1965). *Dark ghetto: Dilemmas of social power*. Middletown, CT: Wesleyan University Press.

Collins, M. (1992). *Ordinary children, extraordinary teachers*. Charlottesville, VA: Hampton Roads Publishing Company, Inc.

Comer, J. P., & Poussaint, A. F. (1992). *Raising Black children: Two leading psychiatrists confront the educational, social, and emotional problems facing Black children*. New York: Penguin Books.

Cone, J. K. (1996). Appearing acts: Creating readers in a high school English class. In *Dealing with diversity: Ensuring success for every student* (pp. 1–24). Cambridge: Harvard Educational Review.

Corbin, S. K., & Pruitt, R. L. III. (1999). Who am I? The development of the African American male identity. In V. C. Polite & J. E. Davis (Eds.), *African American males in school and society: Practices and policies for effective education*. (pp. 68–80). New York: Teachers College Press.

Cummins, J. (1986). Empowering minority students: A framework for intervention. *Harvard Educational Review, 56* (1), 18–36.

Cunningham, P. M., & Allington, R. L. (1999). *Classrooms that work: They can all read and write* (2nd ed.). New York: Addison Wesley Longman.

Darder, A. (1991). *Culture and power in the classroom*. New York: Bergin & Garvey.

Davis, J. E., & Jordan, W. J. (1995). The effects of school context, structure, and experiences on African American males in middle and high school. *Journal of Negro Education*, 63(4), 570–587.

Delpit, L. (1995). *Other people's children: Cultural conflict in the classroom*. New York: The New Press.

Diamond, S. A. (1996). *Anger, madness, and the daimonic*. New York: State University of New York Press.

Drew, D. (1996). *Aptitude revisited: Rethinking math and science education for America's next century*. Baltimore: The John Hopkins University Press.

Dupuis, J. (1999). California lawsuit notes unequal access to AP courses. *Rethinking Schools Online, 14(1)*.

Eggen, P., & Kauchak, D. (2001). *Educational psychology: Windows on classrooms* (5th ed). Upper Saddle River, NJ: Merrill.

Fields, M. V., & Spangler, K. L. (2000). *Let's begin reading right: A developmental approach to emergent literacy* (4th ed). Upper Saddle River, NJ: Merrill.

Fleming, J. E. (1976). *The lengthening shadow of slavery*. Washington: Howard University Press.

Flesch, R. (1955). *Why Johnny can't read and what you can do about it*. New York: Harper & Brothers.

Flores, B., Tefft-Cousins, P., & Diaz, E. (1991). Transforming deficit myths about learning, language, and culture. *Language Arts, 68,* 369–378.

Floyd, C. (1995). *African American high school seniors*. Unpublished doctoral dissertation. Claremont Graduate University, Claremont, CA.

Ford, D. (1995). Desegregating gifted education: A need unmet. *Journal of Negro Education,* 64(1), 53–62.

Fordham, S. (1988). Racelessness as a factor in Black students' school success: Pragmatic strategy or Pyrrhic victory? *Harvard Educational Review, 58* (1), 54–84.

Foster, M., & Peele, T. B. (1999). Teaching Black males: Lessons from the experts. In V. C. Polite & J. E. Davis (Eds.), *African American males in school and society: Practices and policies for effective education* (pp. 8–19). New York: Teachers College Press.

Garbarino, J., Dubrow, N., Kostelny, K., & Pardo, C. (1992). *Children in danger: Coping with the consequences of community violence*. San Francisco: Jossey-Bass Publishers.

Gillet, J. W., & Temple, C. (2000). *Understanding reading problems: Assessment and instruction* (5th ed). New York: Longman.

Gould, S. J. (1981). *The mismeasure of man*. New York: W. W. Norton & Co.

Gunning, T. (2000). *Creating literacy instruction for all children*. Needham Heights, MA: Allyn & Bacon.

Haberman, M. (1995). *Star teachers of children in poverty*. West Lafayette, IN: Kappa Delta Pi.

Hacker, A. (1992). *Two nations: Black and White, separate, hostile, unequal*. New York: Ballantine Books.

Hale, J. E. (1986). *Black children: Their roots, culture, and learning styles* (Rev. ed.). Baltimore: The Johns Hopkins University Press.

Hare, N., & Hare, J. (1991). *The miseducation of the Black child*. San Francisco: Banneker Books.

Harris, A. J. & Sipay, E. R. (1990). *How to increase reading ability: A Guide to developmental and remedial methods*.

Haycock, K. (1998). Good teaching matters: How well-qualified teachers can close the gap. *Thinking K–16*, 3(2), 1–2.

Honig, B. (1999). Reading the right way: What research and best practices say about eliminating failure among beginning readers. In *Reading reading research anthology: The why? of reading instruction* (pp. 7–12). Novato, CA: Consortium on Reading Excellence, Inc., Arena Press.

Hooks, B. (1989). *Talking back*. Boston: South End Press.

Hurd, E., Moore, C., & Rogers, R. (1995). Quiet success: Parenting strengths among African Americans. *Families in Society*, 76(7), 434–443.

Ingersoll, R. M. 1999. The problem of underqualified teachers in American secondary schools. *Educational Researcher*, 28(2), 26–37.

Indrisano, R., & Chall, J. (1995). Literacy development. *Journal of Education*, 177(1), 63–82.

Johnson, K. R. (1969). The language of black children: Instructional implications. In R. L. Green (Ed.), *Racial crisis in American education*. Chicago: Follet Educational Corporation.

Joseph, J. (1996). School factors and delinquency: A study of African American youths. *Journal of Black Studies*, 26(3), 340–355.

Judd, C. M., Smith, E. R., & Kidder, L. H. (1991). *Research methods in social relations* (6th ed.). Fort Worth: Harcourt Brace Jovanovich College Publishers.

Kerlinger, F. N. (1986). *Foundations of behavioral research* (3rd ed.). Fort Worth: Harcourt Brace Jovanovich College Publishers.

Kozol, J. (1986). *Illiterate American*. New York: Penguin Books.

Krashen, S. (1993). *The power of reading: Insights from the research*. Englewood, CO: Libraries Unlimited, Inc.

Kunjufu, J. (1985). *Countering the conspiracy to destroy Black boys*. Chicago: African American Images.

Kunjufu, J. (1990). *Countering the conspiracy to destroy Black boys* (Vol. lll). Chicago: African American Images.

Labov, W. (1972). *Language in the inner city: Studies in the Black English vernacular*. Philadelphia: University of Pennsylvania Press.

Ladson-Billings, G. (1994). *The dreamkeepers: Successful teachers of African-American children*. San Francisco: Jossey-Bass Publishers.

Mabie, G. E. (2000). Race, culture, and intelligence: An interview with Asa G. Hilliard III. *The Educational Forum*, 64 (Spring), 243–251.

Manzo, K. K. (1997a, February). Phonics is back: California ditches whole language texts and returns to the basics. *Teacher* 10–11.

Manzo, K. K. (1997b). Study stresses role of early phonics instruction. *Education Week*, 15(24), 1 and 24.

McAdoo, H. (1992). Upward mobility and parenting in middle-income Black families. In A. K. H. Burlew, W. C. Banks, H. McAdoo, & D. A. Azibo (Eds.), *African American Psychology* (pp. 63–86). California: SAGE Publications.

Mitchell, J. (1982). Reflections of a Black social scientist: Some struggles, some doubts, some hopes. *Harvard Educational Review, 52* (1), 27–44.

Morgan, H. (1980, January–February). How schools fail Black children. *Social Policy*, 49–54.

Murray, C. (1996). Estimating achievement performance: A confirmation bias. *Journal of Black Psychology, 22* (1), 67–85.

National Center for Education Statistics: *Digest of education statistics 1996.* (pp. 187, 208, 211, 224, 286). NCES 96-133. Washington: U.S. Department of Education.

National Center for Education Statistics: *Digest of education statistics 1999.* Washington: U.S. Department of Education.

National Center for Education Statistics. (1999). *The nation's report card.* Washington: U.S. Department of Education.

National Center for Education Statistics: *Digest of education statistics 2000.* Washington: U.S. Department of Education.

National Institute on Drug Abuse. (2000). Washington: National Center for Health Statistics, Substance Abuse and Mental Health Service Administration, Office of Applied Studies.

National Vital Statistics Reports. (1999, October 25). Vol. 47, No. 26.

Nieto, S. (2000). *Affirming diversity: The sociopolitical context of multicultural education* (3rd ed). New York: Longman.

Oakes, J. (1990). *Lost talent: The Underrepresentation of women, minorities and disabled students in science.* Santa Monica, CA: The Rand Corporation.

Oakes, J. (1999). Limiting students' school success and life chances: The impact of tracking. In A. C. Ornstein & L. S. Behar-Horenstein (Eds.), *Contemporary issues in curriculum* (2nd ed.) pp. 224–237. Needham Heights, MA: Allyn and Bacon.

Orange, C., & Horowitz, R. (1999, September). An academic standoff: Literacy task preferences of African and Mexican American male adolescents versus teacher-expected preferences. *Journal of Adolescent and Adult Literacy,* 43:1, 28–39.

Payne, R. K. (1998). *A framework for understanding poverty.* Highlands, TX: RFT Publishing Co.

Polite, V. C. (1999). Combating educational neglect in suburbia: African American males and mathematics. In V. C. Polite & J. E. Davis (Eds.), *African American Males in School and Society: Practices and Policies for Effective Education.* (pp. 97–107). New York: Teachers College Press.

Poplin, M., & Weeres, J. (1992). *Voices from the inside: A report on schooling from inside the classroom.* The Institute for Education in Transformation at the Claremont Graduate School, Claremont, CA.

Quality Counts. (2000, January 13). *Education Week* XlX(18).

Queen, J. A. (1999). *Curriculum practice in the elementary and middle school.* Upper Saddle River, NJ: Prentice Hall.

Roe, B. D., Stoodt, B. D., & Burns, P. C. (1998). *Secondary school literacy instruction: The content areas* (6th ed). Boston: Houghton Mifflin Co.

Rosenblatt, L. M. (1995). *Literature as exploration* (5th ed.). New York: The Modern Language Association.

Routman, R. (1996). *Literacy at the crossroads: Critical talk about reading, writing, and other teaching dilemmas.* Portsmouth, NH: Heinemann.

Ruddell, R. B. (1999). *Teaching children to read and write: Becoming an influential teacher* (2nd ed.). Boston: Allyn and Bacon.

Shannon, P. (1992). Reading instruction and social class. In P. Shannon (Ed.), *Becoming political: Readings and writings in the politics of literacy education* (pp. 128–138). Portsmouth, NH: Heinemann.

Smith, F. (1986). *Insult to intelligence: The bureaucratic invasion of our classrooms.* Portsmouth, NH: Heinemann.

Smitherman, G. (1977). *Talkin' and testifyin': The language of Black America.* Detroit: Wayne State University Press.

Thomas, G. E. (1987). Black students in U.S. graduate and professional schools in the 1980s: A national and institutional assessment. *Harvard Educational Review, 57*(3), 261–279.

Thompson, G. (1998a). Reading to survive: Exploring the coping strategies of African Americans. *Claremont Reading Conference 62nd Yearbook,* pp. 115–125.

Thompson, G. (1998b). *Predictors of resilience in African American adults.* Unpublished doctoral dissertation. The Claremont Graduate University, Claremont, CA.

Thompson, G. (2000). California educators discuss the reading crisis. *The Educational Forum, 64* (Spring), 229–234.

U.S. Census Bureau. (2000). Fedstats. Washington.

U.S. Department of Education. *Digest of Education Statistics* (2000). Washington: National Center for Education Statistics.

U.S. Department of Education. *Digest of Education Statistics* (1999). Washington. National Center for Education Statistics.

U.S. Department of Education. (2000). *National Assessment of Educational al Progress, NAEP Trends in Academic Progress,* various years. Washington: National Center for Education Statistics.

U.S. Departments of Education and Justice. (1999). *Indicators of school crime and safety.* Washington.

U.S. Department of Health. (2000). Washington.

Wenglinsky, H. (2000). *How teaching matters: Bringing the classroom back into discussions of teacher quality.* Princeton: Educational Testing Service.

White, J. L., & Parham, T. A. (1990). *The psychology of Blacks: An African American perspective* (2nd ed.). Upper Saddle River, NJ: Prentice-Hall, Inc.

Wiles, J., & Bondi, J. (1998). *Curriculum development: A guide to practice* (5th ed.). Upper Saddle River, NJ: Prentice Hall, Inc.

Wilson, A. N. (1987). *The developmental psychology of the Black child* (6th ed.). New York: Africana Research Publications.

Wilson, K. R., & Allen, W. R. (1987). Explaining the educational attainment of young Black adults: Critical familial and extra-familial influences. *Journal of Negro Education, 56* (1), 64–76.

Wilson, W. J. (1996). *When work disappears: The world of the new urban poor.* New York: Alfred A. Knopf, Inc.

Wolf, L. E. (1995). *Models of excellence: The baccalaureate origins of successful European American women, African American women, and Latinas.* Unpublished doctoral dissertation. The Claremont Graduate University, Claremont, CA.

Index

African American, critical mass, 16, 67–68; culture 32, 61, 68, 134, 167; males, 32, 39–42, 44, 53–54, 60–61, 63, 141–142; self-esteem, concept, or self-identity, 60–62, 66

Biracialism, 6, 7, 14, 39, 94–95, 134

Clark, Kenneth B., 161, 162, 164
College, 8, 9, 10, 11, 14, 25; attendance rates, 5; plans for 51, 53, 74, 123–132
Columbine Tragedy, 144–146, 149
Comer, James, 3, 16, 60–62; 133–135, 152, 158
Community of Learners, 32, 67
Counselors, school, 98, 126–127, 131–132
Course, failure, 79, 85, 109, 110
Cultural awareness, 68; conflicts, 4
Curriculum, 62, 66, 72, 78, 104, 126; watered down, 63, 129, 130, 131

Deficit views, 3, 19
Delpit, Lisa, 16, 67–68, 133, 150, 152 ; skills and other dilemmas, 28, 32, 43; parent involvement, 156, 158

Discipline, 63, 64, 66, 71, 72, 73; problems, 77, 93, 108, 132; referrals, 24, 52, 64–66, 73, 149
Discrimination, 7. *See also* Racism
Drew, David, E., 86, 93, 124
Dyslexia, 23, 24, 27

Expulsion, 93, 148
Expectations. *See* Teachers

Foster, Michele, 4, 32, 43
Fourth grade, 17, 18, 27, 63; failure syndrome, 4, 18, 74

Garbarino, James, 5, 165
Grade point average, 94, 111, 112, 116, 117
Grade inflation, 8, 108, 140, 163

Haberman, Martin, 31, 45, 67, 77, 149, 152
Hacker, Andrew, 133, 135, 164
Hale, Janet, 4, 19
Harassment, 6, 7, 10, 74; sexual, 146–147
Hilliard, Asa, 62, 68, 140, 159, 162, 164

Homework, 45, 55, 62, 75, 105, 114–
116; benefits, 107, 119, 132; elementary school, 107; high school,
113–116; middle school, 82–83,
86–87

Inequality (of educational opportunity), 29, 56, 105
Instructional practices, 66

Kunjufu, Jawanza, 61–63, 164

Ladson-Billings, Gloria, 32, 43, 62, 67–
68, 150; parent involvement, 159;
successful teachers, 162, 164, 165
Literacy, 17–29

McAdoo, Harriett, 134–135, 156
Media, 62

National Assessment of Educational
Progress, 18, 91, 92
Nieto, Sonia, 133, 135

Oakes, Jeannie, 135, 164

Parent involvement, 11, 23, 25, 60,
104, 128; during elementary
school, 153–154; during high
school, 155; during middle school,
154–155; and school safety, 145
Parham, Thomas, 4, 60–62, 67, 134,
158, 164
Payne, Ruby, 61, 150
Phonics, 23, 25, 28
Polite, Vernon C., 92, 124, 162, 164
Poplin, Mary, 133, 152, 153
Post traumatic stress disorder, 5
Poussaint, Alvin, 3, 16, 60–62; 133–
135, 152, 158
Poverty, 4, 5, 6, 45, 61, 77
Pregnancy, teen, 11, 93, 106

Racism, 3, 12, 22, 52, 60, 65–68; expe-
riences with, 71–72, 102, 107, 133–
140
Reading, 91; scores 91–92. *See also*
Literacy
Resiliency, 15, 98, 151, 165
Retention, grade, 23, 51, 54, 61, 63,
111

Standardized tests, 12, 126, 130, 131
Substance abuse, 6, 9, 11, 14, 15, 93
Suspension, school, 63, 93, 142, 148,
149

Teacher(s): African American, 34, 52,
67–69, 77, 101; characteristics, 32–
33, 43, 70–71, 76, 77; "best," 34, 35–
36, 50, 69–71, 75–77; expectations,
8, 13, 61–63, 68, 103–108, 131; successful, 31, 32, 44, 67; underprepared, 28, 34, 59–60, 93, 124,
132, "worst," 36–37, 54, 71–75, 76–
77, 101–102, 118
Teacher education programs, 43,
167
Teaching methods, culturally relevant, 32, 62
Thompson, Gail L., 15, 28, 134, 92,
151, 165
Tracking, 3, 4, 15, 16, 43, 55–56; effects of, 61, 91, 105–108; and racism, 135

Urban: areas, 5; schools, 63

Violence, 61–62, 67, 141–150

Weeres, Joe, 133, 152, 153
White, Joseph L., 4, 60–62, 67, 134,
158, 164
Whole language, 28
Wilson, William J., 4, 135

ABOUT THE AUTHOR

GAIL L. THOMPSON is Associate Professor, School of Educational Studies, Claremont Graduate University.